A. HAROLD FIELDS

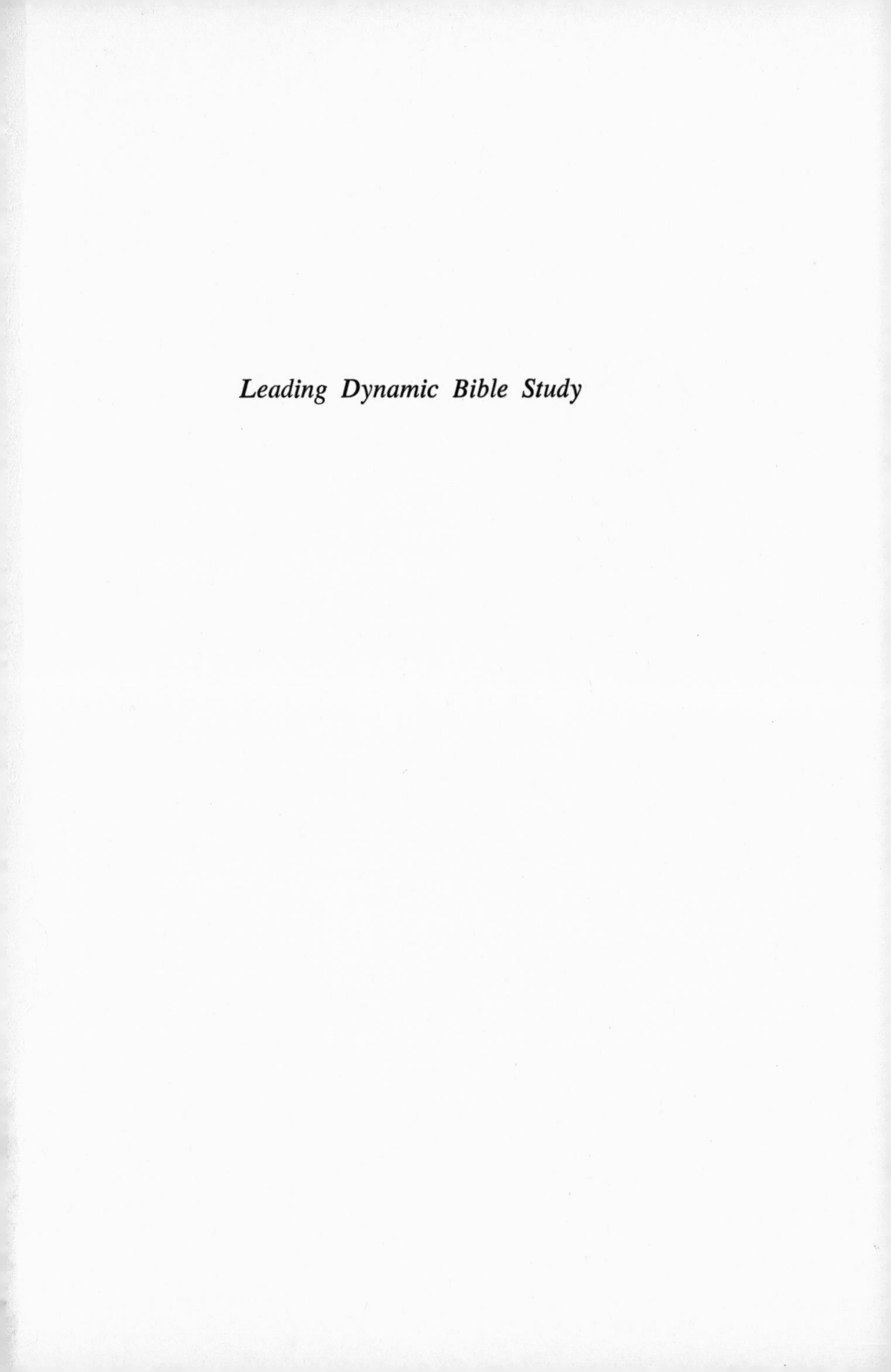

Leading Dynamic Bible Study

LEADING DYNAMIC BIBLE STUDY

Rice A. Pierce

Foreword by Gaines S. Dobbins

BROADMAN PRESS
NASHVILLE, TENNESSEE

To Louise

422–380

Library of Congress catalog card number: 74–78835
Printed in the United States of America

Introduction

Library shelves are crowded with books dealing with the teacher, the learner, the teaching-learning process. Relatively recently has there been concentration of concern on the teacher as a member of a dynamic learning group and education as group process. Literature in this field has been confined largely to the college level.

Dr. Pierce seeks to bring group theory and practice to the service of Bible study. He removes the teacher from his traditional position as active instructor of a passive class and makes him leader of guided dialogue in which members of the group become, in a sense, their own teachers. A *dynamic* group is more than an aggregate of individuals constituting a class. A group becomes dynamic when there is creative interaction that results in change. In this kind of group, as Reuel Howe asserts in *The Miracle of Dialogue,* Jesus Christ joins the group, the Holy Spirit gives guidance, and the Bible "comes alive."

This concept of Bible study does not lessen the importance and responsibility of the teacher. He is the indispensable leader and must know his subject-matter; but his concern is not to "get across" the "lesson" to recipients of his "message," but to involve members of the group in purposeful search for Bible truth relevant to life here and now. The teacher's preparation will thus have two foci—Bible content and responsive persons.

The author would have the teacher-leader avoid the error of merely evoking haphazard talk sometimes disguised as the "discussion method." To this end, the teacher must *plan* to secure group involvement, with clearly defined aims based on biblical content and interests and needs of the group. Varied approaches will be canvassed and the one selected that appears most appropriate. It is at this point that the author makes one of his most valuable contributions in listing and minutely describing the many possibilities of fresh and stimulating approaches to group-centered Bible study.

Does the group-centered concept rule out lecture? Not at all. The teacher will present needed facts and truths, he will stimulate inquiry, he will pave the way for intelligent questions and participation following the exposition; yet the statements should be directed to the group with a view to their reaction and involvement.

The principle of leadership coupled with group participation applies throughout the discussion method. The teacher will not dominate nor will he abdicate. Discussion to be effective should be spontaneous yet structured, informal yet directed. Excellent guidance is given in the book as to how this balance may be achieved.

The inevitable closing chapter on evaluating results departs significantly from the familiar pattern of "tests and measurements." A valuable innovation in the effort to appraise the worth of the teaching-learning experience is enlistment of class cooperation. Who better than the members are qualified to judge the effectiveness and fruitfulness of their Bible study? Three main factors come under critical judgment: the teacher, the learners, the results. What did the prepared teacher do so that the responsive class reacted so that changes occurred? Teacher and class together review the teacher's personality, preparedness, and procedures as these factors impinged on the group. Teacher and class likewise review the members' appreciation, participation, and creative interaction so that their Bible study made a difference. This polarity of teacher-class examination of experiences is continued in case-study fashion until points of strength and weakness are disclosed, always with a view to improvement. This constructive criticism of the joint procedure of teacher and class is applied in detail to varied aspects of the Bible study experiences to the two-fold end that recall may bring enrichment and review may bring improvement.

To the question, Of the methods described, which is best of all? the inferred answer would be that there is no one *best* method—the choice depends on a number of circumstances. Should the question be, Which is the worst? the implied answer is, the method that secures the least class involvement. To this I would venture to add that the poorest method is the one used all the time!

While the writing is remarkably free from academic jargon, the perceptive reader will realize that the author has a sound underlying theology, philosophy, and psychology of education. He assumes a living, acting Triune God who has disclosed himself in the biblical revelation; the center about which he gathers his educational philosophy is the dynamic responsive group made up of individuals who are changed through interaction; and his psychology of education views every person as a universe of potentialities that can be actualized by exposure to divine truth in the framework of life situations.

I am especially gratified that the author has put into practice and now into print ideas which were initiated in a seminar on Group Dynamics that I was privileged to lead in Southern Baptist Theological Seminary.

GAINES S. DOBBINS
Birmingham, Alabama

Acknowledgments

To friends both in the Education Division and the Publishing Division of the Baptist Sunday School Board who encouraged me to develop into printed form the teaching concepts and methods descriptions set forth in this book.

To the many Bible class and Training Union members whose responsiveness helped me to gain confidence in the value of group study processes.

To the Sunday School teachers and other church study leaders in clinics and other conferences who have expressed supportive appreciation for the Bible study approaches illustrated in this book.

To Dr. A. V. Washburn, secretary of the Sunday School Department, Baptist Sunday School Board, whose continued encouragement throughout the evolving of this book confirmed my sense of the worthwhileness of this project.

To Dr. Gaines S. Dobbins, whose teaching and example started me upon the road of leading classroom study through thought-provoking group interaction.

To Dr. William M. Alexander, who helped develop the idea of preparing a teacher-training outline of book-length potential during a course in curriculum building at Peabody College.

Contents

1

How Bible Study Can Be Dynamic

If God is not dead, why does he not speak to a confused, revolutionary world in upheaval?

God does speak to man today, and in many ways. But until man knows what God has said in his written revelation, the Bible, he is not likely to understand God's message through other media. Thus appears the crucial importance of Bible study: to discover God's basic word to man, to understand and appreciate this word, to embrace with conviction the divine truth discovered, and to begin applying this truth in all of life's relationships.[1]

Two Ways to Study the Bible

The Scriptures may be studied in a ceremonial, mechanical, dull, now-we-are-in-Sunday-School manner. Or you—the teacher—and the class may study the Bible in a dynamic manner. You and your class may plumb the very depths of mind and heart, together, as you seek to know and do God's will through study of the written revelation. This spiritual experience together may be called *dynamic Bible study*.

Cannot dynamic Bible study be achieved alone? Yes, to a degree. And it is true that your class members learn as individuals. As individuals they respond to the call of God. But joining with others in thought-provoking, soul-searching Bible study exercises a unique mental and emotional influence upon one. Compare being in the middle of fellow cheering fans at a football game. How different this is from sitting in the end zone all alone! [2]

In a group, Bible study takes on a new dimension. More than one meaning lies in Christ's promise to be present when two or three per-

---

[1] See, also, Findley B. Edge, *Teaching for Results* (Nashville: Broadman Press, 1956), pp. 65–66.

[2] See, also, Sara Little, *Learning Together in the Christian Fellowship* (Richmond: John Knox Press, 1961), pp. 14 ff.

sons gather to seek and do his will (Matt. 18:20). A dynamic activity begins when these minds and hearts focus intently upon a passage of God's Word and the Holy Spirit charges this spiritual activity with power!

How Bible Study Becomes Dynamic

What deeply moving experience comes to one as he moves from his private study, reflection, and prayer to the time of classroom Bible study? The desire to grow spiritually and follow Christ has led your class members to private study and prayer. Yet, when one has gained new knowledge and new insights from this private study, he still knows these are only his own prayerfully gained insights. He realizes that these beliefs still need to be tried out on *people.* These opinions need to be applied to everyday relationships with others. Then he can feel more assured that his insights are valid and can be developed into skills for Christian living.

Small-group, classroom Bible study thus *interprets, refines,* and serves as a *check* on individual study efforts. Placing facts and views on Bible truth alongside those of the teacher and other class members helps the individual clarify his thinking. He discovers what he actually thinks as he voices his ideas about what the Bible means. He also learns to think straighter as he and others hear what he is saying. A person's learning in the class group thus is realistic: he learns in relation to others with whom he must live. It is like continually fitting a shoe to the foot as the shoe is made. The completed shoe will fit far more successfully than if this continual reference of shoe to foot had not been made.

As a person engages with others in Bible study under the teacher's leadership, he profits also from what *the teacher and others learn.* Thus he gains more balanced points of view. He learns to evaluate his own ideas as he comes to respect even the conflicting views of others. And he learns to withhold judgment for a while.

Another learning skill which Bible study in a small group helps one to acquire is how to do *concentrated thinking.* He becomes able to pick out more quickly just what is being said in the group. He finds himself reacting to the teacher and others more quickly and more accurately. By studying with others, he thus gains increasing ability to see spiritual truth as it is. This gives him overall confidence in communicating biblical insights and convictions with others—

valuable skill for living with, and witnessing to, other human beings.

One deeper value of taking part in a Bible study group is that soon a person *understands himself* better. He is influenced to use the Bible and think through his own problems as others in the class discuss theirs. In becoming accepted by the class as a person with problems, he has less to hide. He becomes free to grow—to analyze himself, to recognize and to acknowledge weak spots, to seek solutions. And he soon discovers that he does have value in the sight of others, that he is not the world's worst mixed up "stupe" after all. This new concept of himself as a sincere, learning person, free and encouraged to grow, becomes a unifying, motivating power in his development. He discards the walls of self-concealment. He walks honestly and gladly before others in a humble resolve to grow spiritually. Soon he feels increased power for understanding, reaching convictions, and taking action.

The *warm fellowship* that the learner finds in class Bible study also aids his spiritual growth. The new friends thus made enrich his life. The old friends which he now comes to know better take on added significance for his life. Now, he understands people better. Knowing how the teacher and others feel—and caring far more about how they feel—he can achieve the reconciliation with others that characterizes the Christian. When class discussion proceeds as it should, deep-seated antagonisms within a person come to light and are dealt with by him. Then he begins to help others in the group find *themselves.*

To change, to grow spiritually, is one's goal as a student of the Bible. He can do this far better in a group of persons with like spiritual purpose than he can do it alone! [3]

Initial Preparation to Teach

Now you are preparing to lead your class in Bible study. What will you do first as you begin to develop a teaching plan?

After you have settled in your best study place with your materials around you, ask Christ's guidance. From this point until the last teaching activity discussed in this book, you will need the ever-present aid of the Holy Spirit. No preparation and no teaching procedure should be undertaken by human skill alone. Teaching the Bible is a

[3] See, also, Malcolm S. and Hulda F. Knowles, *Introduction to Group Dynamics* (New York: Association Press, 1959), pp. 59–62.

divine assignment and will be done successfully only with divine assistance.

The first thing you want to know is: How does this study relate to the ones just completed and to those yet to come in the unit? Ask yourself questions like: Will I need to be careful not to let us simply repeat what we have already studied? Do I need to watch out lest we overlap too far what we shall be studying two or three sessions from now? How do the suggested teaching aims in the teacher's materials appear to support each other? What seems to be the chief spiritual issue in the Scriptures which the curriculum highlights for this session?

This brief taking of your bearings will help you to make your background preparation more selectively.

The Bible Passages

The first study you may want to do now is to read carefully the relevant passages of Scripture. Suppose the topic for study is "Developing Christian Relationships in the Home" and the specific Scripture passages are 2 Samuel 15:1–12 and 18:31–33. No doubt the reflective reading of all six chapters, 2 Samuel 13–18, will help you understand best the relationship which developed in the home between David and his son Absalom. In fact, also reading chapters 11–12 will offer you valuable background for helping the class better understand David as a father.

After reading the specific passage for study and the larger or basic Scripture background, you now are ready to concentrate on the passages selected for special class study. You can see that these verses form an excellent base from which to seek biblical guidance on the subject of family relationships. Read these fifteen verses again carefully. Jot down on a sheet of paper any comments or questions which "jump out" at you from these passages as being especially appropriate for class members to consider. This list of ideas, questions, or problems will grow as your preparation continues and focuses on your teaching aim. It will form the raw material out of which your completed teaching plan later will emerge.

The Class Members' Material

Now notice what the writer of the class members' material has said about these passages. He had before him the same Bible study outlines and suggested teaching aim which the writers of your more extensive teacher's guide possessed. Yet he was given less space in which to write, and his viewpoint may have been quite different from what you would have expected. What he says, therefore, may enrich your insights into the Bible passages.

Moreover, this material is what your class members will be studying. Read it, for you want to know as much as they do about the Bible passages! And you want to prepare to react to members' questions and comments about statements in their materials. Too, you may plan to enlist their thinking upon especially significant interpretations found in their quarterly. This attention on your part to their own study material can increase significantly the attention which they themselves will pay to it. Here, then, is one good solution to the problem of how to get class members to prepare for class Bible study: Know enough about their material each Sunday that they can see your respect for, and use of, it in class discussion.

As a result of reading the class members' material, then, you may discover several important questions, issues, or problems. Remember, though, that these are just "good possibilities" for concentrated class thinking. You haven't decided yet to use them. A lot more study, prayer, and reflection must take place yet.

The Teacher's Guide

As a matter of fact, you probably recognize that your preparation for teaching has only begun. Only now are you about to study more closely the meaning of the Bible passages. In your teacher's quarterly or guide, the ten or more verses selected for close study usually are explained. Here is where you let the Bible and its real meaning speak more clearly to you.

As you discover more of the Scriptures' real meaning, you think of more penetrating questions with which to challenge your class members' thinking and attitudes. For instance, after merely reading 2 Samuel 15:12 you may have written down for class deliberation a rather inaccurate question, such as, Did Absalom think he could so easily persuade Ahithophel to join him? But after reading the member's material and certainly your teacher's guide, you know that a better question might be this: What kind of plotting against his father do you think Absalom must have done in order thus to have gotten Ahithophel to come so quickly to him? The point here is that the germ of a good class study question can arise just from reading a passage in the Bible. But the question which finally can be placed before the class for careful thought and decision often must come only after a close study of the passage plus the exposition of trusted Bible scholars.

Other Study Resources

This thought brings us to the fact that other study helps also may have been prepared to interpret the outlines you are using. One-volume comments on the quarter's studies often will help you. For instance, the Uniform outlines used by many churches have inspired the preparation of several teaching guides in book form. And some denominations have prepared teachers' aids to supplement the regular quarterly teaching guides.

Larger commentaries often are helpful in determining the meaning of a difficult, a disputed, or a neglected verse, phrase, or word. If the writers of the members' and the teachers' material have followed the suggested thrust of the topic, key phrases and verses should be thoroughly dealt with there. But such is not always the case. Or you may feel led of the Holy Spirit to phrase your own different teaching aim. In this event, you may wish to develop verses or phrases in the Scripture passage which your teacher's quarterly does not give much attention to. In this and in other cases, you will find a sound multivolume Bible commentary quite helpful. Single volumes on one book of the Bible serve this same purpose of offering concentrated study on each significant verse, phrase, and word in the passage.

Other types of reading, of course, enter into your personal preparation for teaching. The type of study which we have been considering may have been going on over a period of days. In this time you have gotten the feel of the content, become involved in the father-son relationship (David and Absalom), thought about why nations decay and invite revolution, and so on. Thus you already may have seen what may be quite relevant material in newspapers, magazines, non-religious books, motion pictures, television shows, radio reports, and in other daily news media. Society today offers full illustration of the rebellion of youth against the adult world. This kind of research is important if you are planning to lead your class in Bible study which is relevant to their time and needs. And this kind of reading no doubt will continue right up to class time with the latest newspaper and radio report illustrating the seriousness and significance of these Bible passages.

Your Need for a Teaching Aim

You may say at this point: With all this Bible study that I have done, why do I need a teaching aim? Why can't I just teach the Bible? By all means you will "teach the Bible"—or teach *class members* the Bible. But what will you do with all the Scripture passages listed for use in this session? Grind through word by word and verse by verse—until time runs out? Avoid the issue by spending all your time talking about how people lived in Bible times? Pick out the easy, familiar verses and "preach" on them? Select a real problem verse or concept and run out the class time letting members argue and conjecture over this?

Admittedly, this is a good question: What will you do with the brief, highly selective Scripture passages listed as the basis for class Bible study?

The answer to this question is *aim-guided teaching*. For if you do not have a teaching aim clearly in mind, any grouping of Scripture passages can seem like a confusing conglomeration of Bible verses. These verses are rich Bible truth, yes, but to what end next Sunday, and the next, and the next? How are they chosen and what spiritual purpose do they serve? Aim-guided teaching means prayerfully deciding what purpose these verses are to serve in your class Bible study and then, again with the Holy Spirit's guidance, teaching in a way to achieve this outcome.

How do you arrive at selecting this aim which is so important for your teaching?

The Central Truth of the Passages

You have completed your initial study of the Bible material for the next class session. No doubt you have noticed in the teacher's guide or other resource books a summary of 2 Samuel 15:1–12 and 18:31–33, which we are using as the proposed passages for our own discussion purposes. You also can know by now the central truth of these passages. Suppose this summary statement of scriptural truth in terms significant for young adult class members reads something like this: A young adult who selfishly seeks his own interests and advancement at the expense of parents, family group, and God's ways sooner or later comes to tragic consequences in all of his relationships.

If you are teaching older adults, perhaps the central truth of the passages in terms of your class members' deepest spiritual concerns will read like this: Parents who subordinate the nurture of their God-entrusted children to pursuing secondary aims can expect tragic consequences to result in relationships with their children. However this central truth is worded, this statement becomes the scriptural basis for the aim which will guide your preparation and teaching of the class.

The Spiritual Concerns of Class Members

Phrasing your teaching aim thus requires you to identify clearly the thrust of the Bible passages for your class members today. Stating this central truth then leads you to think in a concentrated way about your members. Just what are they thinking about? What are they ready to learn, to focus attention upon? They most certainly have questions, strong inner desires, intellectual leanings and needs which have much to do with what and how they will learn the Bible truth you will be helping them to consider.

At this point you may say: It's quite true that, in planning class discussion in a certain direction around the Bible passages, I want to keep in mind my members' chief spiritual concerns. But how do I know what these concerns are? How do I keep from still spraying broadside "in the dark" just as if I had no teaching aim?

First, *ask yourself questions like these:* What occupies their daily thoughts the most? What will they come to class most preoccupied about? What problems are they wrestling with right now? In some way, with the leadership of God's Spirit, you can help your members to find assistance with these concerns through study of the selected Bible passages.

Then, find out just what does concern your class members by *talking with them individually*. Pick out two or three members whom you sense need particular help right now. Ask them to help you give the class discussion next time a relevant, profitable emphasis. You are asking them frankly to help you shape the class discussion in a direction which they feel is timely. You don't have to cause them to feel that you are trying specifically to meet their needs. This implication might be too personal for some members. But as you genuinely ask them, and as they genuinely respond to you, you may be sure that some of their most personal interests and concerns will come to you.

You also can talk generally with individual members during the week. Find out what is causing them the most concern. Make no reference, perhaps, to next Sunday morning. The Holy Spirit will help you later to decide what concerns need most to be faced with God's Word at class time.

Personal conversation, telephone calls, letters, shortwave radio—all these and other ways have been used by teachers to discover the deep spiritual concerns of their class members.

But you also have available to you such opportunities as *class meetings* for discovering what members feel they need most from the study of God's Word. You already may be having a class meeting once a month to help maintain Christian fellowship, plan witnessing and ministering projects, and so on. If this is true, you also may use this time to ask members what they feel to be some essential areas to take up in class as you study successive Bible passages during the month. *Unsigned suggestion slips* offer a good way for members to get some of their most personal concerns into the prayerful, loving range of class ministering. Even a class *"question box"* into which members may quietly and practically unnoticed drop their discussion requests can bring a sure helpfulness to the Bible study which you lead week by week.

Reliable reports from class members, the pastor, and other genuinely interested persons also can let you know what is a pressing concern of persons in the class at a given time. Thus you prayerfully can shape your teaching aim so that this spiritual need may receive help.

Responses to Bible Truth

In phrasing your teaching aim you also should seek to influence the possible responses which you and your class members may make to the instructions God's Word brings you. These responses may be *inner,* positive responses which *individual members* will make as the Holy Spirit speaks to them through the Bible and class discussion. These acts of silent commitment and decision can be tremendously significant for the individuals themselves and eventually for Christ's kingdom work. Or individuals may make *outward* responses in class or soon afterward, as a result of the Bible study which you have led.

In addition to individual responses, you may hopefully expect that your class will be willing to obey Christ in some way as a *group,* following a discovery of Christ's command and class conviction that Christ should be followed. The nature of the Bible passage, the spiritual circumstances in your church and community, the state of members' readiness to follow Christ, and other factors will affect your thinking here.

At any rate, it is here that you may begin thinking about what kind of response you will seek as you state your teaching aim. So let us think further along this line now as we consider the kind of aim which you will use to guide your teaching.

Your Role as Teacher

What is your role as teacher in the class? To bring them "a sermon before the sermon" if you meet on Sunday morning? To teach a "lesson" (instead of teaching persons)? To tell class members what the Bible says (if they will only be quiet and listen)? If you are teaching youth, to "make" them be quiet so you can explain each verse in the selected passages before the bell rings?

You may not accept any of these perhaps unfair descriptions of the teacher's role in class Bible study. Thus far we have assumed that you are considering a joint undertaking which involves you and your class. Together you are studying the Scriptures, with the help of the Holy Spirit. And this concept of Bible teaching is supported by realizing that your class members *already* are engaged willingly in Bible study. By their very presence they say that this is their purpose and their desire.

Your role as teacher thus is to *help* your class members—help them to read, think, and respond to God's Word. A deep sense of Christian ministry and encouragement comes to you as you think of yourself as helping your class members to achieve their own acknowledged purposes in Bible study and obedience to Christ.

Four Kinds of Teaching Aims

Your class members may be said to be engaged in four kinds of learning activities as you lead them in Bible study Sunday by Sunday.

They are gaining *knowledge* of what the Bible says. They are gaining *understanding* of and *appreciation* for what the Bible says. They are developing *convictions* as to the meaning, truthfulness, and value for living of what they are discovering in the Bible. And they are *using* these Bible-based convictions as they come in contact with persons day by day. The one who more or less voluntarily comes to your class for Bible study actually is engaged to some degree in these four kinds of learnings. Other ways of labeling these learning experiences may have certain values, but the processes must generally be the same: gaining knowledge; gaining understanding, appreciations, and attitudes; developing convictions; and applying all these other learnings in life's relationships.

As your class members engage in these learning activities week by week, you are their helper. Thus you have four teaching aims in the course of a several-session unit. Here are examples of all four kinds.

Recall our Scripture passages and topic which were selected for the purpose of illustration. Our passages were 2 Samuel 15:1–12 and 18:31–33. The topic was "Developing Christian Relationships in the Home." Assume for the moment that you are teaching young adults about the ages of twenty-one to twenty-five. You might state the *first* kind of aim something like this: to help class members examine the experiences of Absalom and David in their relationship as son and father. You can see that this is a desired outcome involving the exploring of Bible content.

I

The *second* kind of aim might read: To help class members understand and appreciate the significance of the experiences which Absalom and David had as son and father.

II

The *third* kind of aim might be stated: To help class members, in light of the experiences of Absalom and David, to strengthen their convictions about respecting and loving their parents.

III

The *fourth* kind of teaching aim would read: To help class members decide upon ways by which they will seek to deepen the bonds of respect and affection between themselves and their parents.[4]

IV

These four sample aims will be repeated or referred to from time to time through the book and designated by the roman numerals I–IV, based on the order given above. In summary, aim I seeks to

---

[4] See, also, John T. Sisemore, *Blueprint for Teaching* (Nashville: Broadman Press, 1964), p. 57.

transmit content; aim II seeks to *implant appreciation*; aim III seeks to *develop convictions*; and aim IV seeks to *stimulate action.*

Deciding on Your Aim

What kind of aim will you use in a given session? This depends to a large extent on what you and the class are studying in the unit. For clarity of illustration, assume that you are making a four-session study of son/daughter-parent relationships in a young adult class. You well could use the four teaching aims just stated, and in the same sequence, for usually you do well to place a knowledge, Bible-content aim first. Help the class to find out what the Bible says. Then in the next session help the class to understand passages, to appreciate and to value the biblical insights gained. In the third session you build upon knowledge, understanding, and appreciation to help develop convictions. After members have gained or strengthened their convictions, they are ready for you to help them act toward others in obedience to God's Word.

Of course, one teaching aim does not absolutely rule out all elements of the other three. A class does not have to wait mechanically until the fourth session before beginning to apply divine truth to their home relationships! And even with the third and fourth types of aims, you and the class will be discovering new knowledge of what the Bible says, new understandings and appreciations. But you can see that each of the four kinds of aims demands primary emphasis. This emphasis becomes important later as you prayerfully plan teaching procedures suited to the particular kind of outcome you seek.

Sometimes you and the class have only one or two sessions on an important Bible theme, as your study outlines set forth the topics. It is here that you have to consider all that we have said, plus additional factors, in deciding which of these four types of aims to use. Often you can combine the first two and the last two aims in a two-topic unit. When the outlines you are using cover an important Bible theme in just one session, you may prefer an application-to-life aim. You also would have to deal with facts, meanings, and convictions during class discussion.

It may be, however, that your class members' deepest spiritual concern will help you to decide which type of aim to use in planning for a given session. If members want most to explore Bible content because of special circumstances, this is a strong guide for you. Or what if the church or community situation causes your class to be seriously preoccupied with *what to do* as Christians? You can hardly decide upon the slower-paced aim of exploring Old Testament customs, practices, and events.

Another aid to use in deciding finally what your teaching aim will be is your teacher's guide. Often the curriculum planners have included a possible teaching aim for you to consider using with the selected Bible passages. Of course the writers knew that this printed aim was only suggestive, and maybe quite general. But you may find good help in checking your present thinking with this printed possibility. It usually is arrived at with some of the thoroughness with which you here are approaching your own decision about an aim.

At this point we might do well to decide for ourselves upon a teaching aim for primary use throughout the rest of this book. Whatever we decide that it should be, you will not forget it! For nearly every other phase of teacher preparation, actual teaching, follow-through, and evaluation of your teaching will reflect which kind of aim we have selected.

Recall again the factors which point us in a direction which is almost sure to be spiritually profitable for the class. The *central truth* of the passages we are using may be stated: A person who selfishly seeks his own interests and advancement at the expense of parents, family group, and God's ways sooner or later comes to tragic consequences in all of his relationships. In the absence of specific knowledge of your own members, let us assume that, if they are young adults, their chief *spiritual concerns* in this area of Bible truth cluster around the problem of achieving independence from parents without losing respect and affection for them. Possible *responses to Bible truth* in this study center around members' agreeing upon good ways to foster respect and affection for parents.

Since this is just one book, we prefer a teaching aim which relates best to all the following chapters and yet is a realistic, honestly conceived teaching aim. This factor, plus the preceding three, points us toward the fourth kind of aim: *To help class members decide upon ways by which they will seek to deepen the bonds of respect and affection between themselves and their parents.*

The selection of a personally involving teaching aim takes you and the class well along the road toward dynamic Bible study experiences.

2
Planning for Group Involvement

Your class members learn by exploring the contents of the Bible. They continue the process by gaining understanding and appreciation of Bible truth. Then they try appropriating personally in their thinking and feelings these new biblical insights. They practice applying these insights in daily relationships, then evaluate all these learning experiences. And they repeat this cycle over and over again.

They begin the learning process with dissatisfaction with themselves over their knowledge of God's Word and their obedience to it. Then they discover possibilities in the Scriptures for fulfilling their desire to know God's will better and to do it. They begin practicing what appear to be good ways of responding to Bible truth, and they take careful notice of results. Then they select those insights and ways of expressing Bible truth that seem to accomplish best Christ's revealed purposes and bring deepest satisfaction, and they integrate these practices into their ways of trying to follow Christ.[1] Thus you may regard your class members as *thinkers* as well as learners.

Learning and Teaching Methods

Your role as teacher is to help this kind of thinking and learning to take place through prayerful, creative use of teaching methods which foster these learning experiences. But someone may ask: Why use a "teaching method" at all? Why not just "teach the Bible"?

You can't teach your class without choosing a teaching procedure, can you? Just as well say that you can go from your home to town without choosing a mode of transportation. And so your decision is not, Must I be so artificial as to choose a "teaching method"? Your

---

[1] See, also, Matthew B. Miles, *Learning to Work in Groups* (New York: Teachers' College Publications, 1959), pp. 37–45.

decision of necessity has to be, What teaching approach shall I plan to use during the next class session?

How would you like to see the coach of your favorite football team tell his players on Monday: "Now, boys, we want to get ready to play the best game of our lives next Saturday. I've got just one instruction for you this week. Each afternoon you come out for practice. And when you do, don't clutter up your minds with formations or plays. Just get out there each day and *play football*!" Do you think the coach and team would meet with much success on Saturday? No, and of course you do not think that all you have to do in order to prepare for leading Bible study is just get ready to "teach."

One teacher once expressed himself as if he thought Bible teaching was something like spraying air freshener in the room: All he had to do was spray, and the contents of the bottle would do the rest. It is true that God's Word, no matter how taught if done sincerely, will not return unto him void. But you are not trying for this minimal result as you teach! Christ is counting on you to seek a *maximum* result in the lives of your class members. This maximum result requires that you use a well-thought-out approach.

Here is one important reminder, however, as we begin to think about ways to lead dynamic Bible study. The teaching concepts and procedures which we shall examine presuppose earnest prayer at every turn. They do not take the place of Bible knowledge and deep concern for the spiritual condition of each of your class members. These ways of teaching will not run on their own educational power alone, or on your skill alone. As mentally and emotionally stimulating as these teaching approaches have been found by others to be, you still will need to seek the ever-willing aid of the Holy Spirit if any teaching idea or procedure whatever is to achieve the outcome that you desire.

Using Different Teaching Approaches

Vary your way of teaching from Sunday to Sunday. This varying may not mean a scientifically calculated movement from one procedure to the next week by week. But it does suggest that in the course, say, of a month you will use more than one method of involving your class members in Bible searching, reflection, discussion of biblical meanings, and decision making.

Nor does this idea of varying Bible teaching approaches stem merely from seeking variety for variety's sake. Such motivation would be of the most shallow sort. There are good reasons for using particular teaching methods during certain Bible study sessions.

First, your *teaching aims* often vary in nature from session to session. We have seen that in a four-topic unit, your teaching aim may progress from knowledge to understanding to appreciation, attitude, and conviction to application in life relationships. Certain classroom procedures assist you best in seeking prayerfully to accomplish each of these four teaching aims.

Second, the Bible material often varies in *literary form* and *"temperature"* from session to session. One study will be based on a Psalm, another on Hebrew law, another on a parable of Jesus, another on the highly figurative book of Revelation. Each form of Bible content can be studied better by you and your class when you use classroom study procedures which help best to get at the meaning and spirit of the Bible material. Moreover, when the Bible content is on a "hot" subject for your class members at the moment, certain teaching approaches work best for achieving your teaching aim. When you are studying passages and a topic where members need to have their interest and concern aroused considerably, other procedures help you more.

Third, your *classroom situation* often varies. When the class study situation varies, often your classroom procedure should vary. What are some of these classroom factors which may suggest a different kind of class Bible study approach from the ordinary? *The mood of the members* in recent sessions or during the previous week may suggest to you a certain kind of approach on Sunday morning. What if you are teaching college young people and they have just finished examinations on Friday or Saturday? Or what if the youth in your church are in a rebellious mood toward church leaders? What if a crisis has occurred in the community during the week? What if the young people are discouraged over the apparent hopelessness of developing a stimulating church youth program? Or what if you think some members of a certain temperament are to be in the class this time?

These possibilities illustrate the fact that certain other classroom procedures might help to answer your class members' deep concerns better than just "preaching at" them, asking an endless round of easily answered, factual questions on the Bible passage, or doing what you did last time. And if you suddenly have begun to have a discipline problem in your youth or subteen class, one classroom procedure well may be preferred over another.

The *physical circumstances* of your class situation also may cause you to use a classroom approach different at one time from another. Maybe the class time is going to be short. Instead of the forty minutes you usually count on, you will have only twenty minutes. Or maybe another class is to be placed near yours behind a screen, and your noise must be kept at a minimum (or you know that the other teacher can outtalk you lecturing!).

Moreover, the makeup of your class may vary at times, and the *abilities of class members* thus may vary. On days when certain members are or are not to be present, then class procedures different from the last time may serve best.

Fourth, a change in classroom approach may be needed simply for the *mental and emotional relief* of yourself and your class members. Some procedures can become strenuous! This change is not variety for variety's sake, as you see. It is variety for spiritual health's sake.

Fifth, you and the class may want to *experiment*. Maybe all of you want to find fresh, moving ways to let God's Word speak to you. You may want to discover ways for your members to respond more freely and frankly. They may want you to let them give expression to what they feel about what the passage says. And so both you and the class may want to try out more satisfying ways to engage in class Bible study.

And, finally, you may be able to reflect upon your teaching situation and discover other even more significant reasons for using different Bible-teaching approaches month by month. Not far down your own list could be simply the desire *to broaden and deepen your Bible-teaching skill* for the sake of Christ and of the persons whom he has entrusted to you.

Four Basic Teaching Methods

The four Bible-teaching approaches mentioned here are some of the best ways to provide opportunities for youth and older persons to make the discoveries, gain the understandings and convictions, and arrive at the spiritual decisions that are possible in dynamic Bible study. They provide a balanced cross section of the teaching procedures dealt with in this book.

The names by which these methods are called are not standardized in the field of religious education, of course. And so there is no one way to label such procedures. The names used here seek to be descriptive and thus helpful in this additional respect. By scanning the most-often-used books on leading class or group study, you will recognize some of these teaching approaches under the same or perhaps other names.

These four basic teaching methods are informal discussion, lecture forum, classroom Bible research forum, and formal discussion. By basic is meant here simply a teaching approach which can take all the class time as you teach by it. Also, remember that *no hard and fast line* can be drawn between what approach may at one time be basic for you—that is, may be the procedure you are using almost exclusively on a particular occasion—and a method that you might use to *supplement* your basic teaching approach at the time. But some procedures do take longer than others to use with spiritual profit. Any of these procedures can be adapted and used more briefly, as we shall see later, to supplement another basic, total-session approach that you are using in your teaching plan.

Informal discussion.—As you teach using this approach, you lead the class to think through Bible teachings and implications by asking them carefully phrased questions. These probing, often open-ended questions grow out of the Bible passages to be studied and out of class members' deepest life concerns to which these passages might speak. Your process of teacher preparation leads you finally to select four or five questions that, when thought through reflectively by the class, lead toward achieving your teaching aim for the session.[2]

Lecture forum.—With lecture forum you use some fifteen or twenty minutes (in a thirty- or forty-minute session) to set forth certain biblical facts, interpretations, and implications as the basis for class members' own thinking. Then, using perhaps probing questions or reaction groups, you lead members to react to what you have said, to what the Bible says, and to one another. You conclude the session

---

[2] See, also, J. Jeffery Auer and Henry L. Ewbank, *Handbook for Discussion Leaders* (New York: Harper & Row, 1954), pp. 34–35,74.

by summarizing what has been agreed upon both as to biblical meanings and class response to Bible truth.

Classroom Bible research forum.—This approach to Bible study involves your assigning to individuals, to small groups in the class, or (often) to the whole class a research task to carry out during the first part of the session. Members examine closely the assigned Scripture passages, commentaries, Bible dictionaries, or other resources, using questions or other guidelines by which to explore the materials. Then you and your class members take up the questions or other points of research, hearing reports, discussing interpretations, and agreeing upon general conclusions. Finally, you lead class discussion in the direction of achieving your teaching aim. Often this direction involves agreement as to what God's Word actually says to you individually and as a class, and what you will do.

Formal discussion.—Using this approach, you lead the class members through several well-defined steps to explore a spiritual problem of deep concern to them and one with which the given Bible passages deal. First, you lead members to decide upon the problem in Bible study that they desire most to explore. Sometimes this decision has been made beforehand. Then you help members consider the biblical and other pertinent facts. Next you guide the class in determining possible solutions to the spiritual problem. Then you help everyone consider the advantages and disadvantages of each solution. Finally, you help members select the preferred solution and consider the action they will take in obeying God's Word.

Your Basic Teaching Approach

You have seen that no matter how you help a class engage in Bible study, you use some teaching method, and that varying factors determine what approach you use for a given session. You have also looked briefly at four basic ways of leading Bible study, all of which help persons learn in somewhat distinctive ways.

Now you are ready to consider two good basic approaches for leading the class in a study of our selected Scripture passages for this book, 2 Samuel 15:1–12 and 18:31–33. Notice that we say *two* basic procedures, and ones of different nature. This is in order to illustrate the fact that the basic approach is important, but that the supplementary procedures (chapter 3) also go far toward determining the quality of the class learning experience. For brevity's sake, we shall not expand the method selection process unduly. Our own process of deciding upon a teaching approach basically will follow the considerations discussed earlier in this chapter under "Using Different Teaching Approaches."

First, consider your teaching aim (IV): *To help class members decide upon ways by which they will seek to deepen the bonds of respect and affection between themselves and their parents.* Now note the Scripture passages and their "temperature," the central truth of the passages, the life concerns of young adults (or those of the age group you teach) in this area of Bible study, and life responses which your class members may make as a result of this Bible study. The passages and their basic message are not accusing so as to generate resistance, but they are emotionally moving. Thus their tone seems to work toward achieving your teaching aim. So you choose a basic procedure which lets the Bible's mood at this point become reflected exactly in class discussion. If David had become bitter and had cursed his son at Absalom's death, perhaps you would choose another teaching approach aimed at responding first to David's attitude.

Your members are indeed concerned about their relationships with parents. You are safe in choosing a procedure which invites members to speak freely. All responses may not be favorable to your teaching aim at first, but the deep filial and other spiritual concerns in the class do work favorably for achieving this outcome.

The life responses which you can hope that your class members will make as a result of this Bible study point in the direction of your teaching aim. Therefore, you choose a teaching procedure which expects—indeed helps—members to face up to *actions that they are willing to commit themselves in class to taking* after the Bible study session has ended. Your teaching aim calls for action-response. It goes about as far as it can in getting outside the class session to help members actually do what they say in class they want to do and will do. And so you choose a basic teaching approach which can lead you and the class to this action point by the end of the session.

Which basic teaching approach, then, do you choose? *Informal discussion* seems to offer the most satisfying and purposeful approach to a study of these two Bible passages. The thought-provoking questions which you ask can deal realistically with every type of literary form in these rich passages. And such questions can bring the spiritual problems of your class members strongly under the healing ministry of God's Word. Supplementary procedures complete the effectiveness of informal discussion with this teaching aim.

For an alternate teaching approach, *lecture forum* could be strong. Much biblical background can profitably be introduced as you begin the study. You can offer tentative insights into the personality and character of Absalom and David. The forum period plus supplementary procedures can bring members significantly into the class study experience after—and perhaps during—your exposition. By the time you reach the place in class study where your members decide upon actions they will take, you will be using a member-involving, supplementary procedure.

The unique values in supplementary group study procedures being what they are, other basic teaching approaches of course can be used with spiritual profit. Any basic procedure which brings you and class members individually to grips with the deep spiritual issues of the Scripture passages must of necessity serve well Christ's purposes for the class.

Other Preparation

The mechanic will not begin to overhaul his car without preparing to use a wrench. Just so, you use the chalkboard and other fundamental teaching aids as you work with the Holy Spirit in repairing the spiritual lives of your class members. You increase several times the amount of impression your teaching makes upon members as you use these visual aids. Class members not only hear but they see. Their attention is secured and held. Their thinking is stimulated and guided. Thus you lead class discussion more easily toward the achieving of your teaching aim, and you summarize more clearly.[3]

Nonprojected teaching aids are essential for leading thoughtful Bible study.

The chalkboard.—The chalkboard stands perhaps at the top of the list of those nonprojected teaching aids which broaden and deepen —add a dynamic quality to—the Bible study experience of your class members. You often can adjust to whatever type of chalkboard you have in the room. Whether you have a stationary or a movable board, it needs to stand right in front of your class. If the board is fastened

[3] See, also, LeRoy Ford, *Tools for Teaching and Training* (Nashville: Broadman Press, 1961), pp. 11–14.

on the wall, it is your class which may have to do the moving, of course. Be sure that chalk and an eraser are on hand. The stationary board which is in your room may not be large enough for you to record properly all the responses and organization of thinking which you and your class do during a session. If this is true and you cannot purchase what you need, you may make a chalkboard inexpensively and place it upon a table or an easel.

Newsprint, butcher's paper, or other large white sheets of paper assist you in ways similar to those of the chalkboard. You may use felt markers or crayons for easy reading by the class.

The discussion board (storyboard, planning board, teaching board) also aids you in recording class members' responses and in arranging them for class evaluation. You may prepare such a board by gluing strips of cardboard about six inches apart and lengthwise across a large piece of posterboard or side of a corrugated box. Glue the strips only at the bottom so that you can slip into them 4 by 6 cards on which class members' responses have been written with felt-tip pen or crayon.

Maps, charts, and posters.—Certain Bible study units require you to use maps if you are to teach realistically. Even in describing the movements of Absalom, for instance, as he stirred up rebellion against David, your pointing out place after place on the map increases learning as the plotting of Absalom becomes more vivid. Examine carefully the type of maps available to you before your class secures one. You and the class may decide upon a map for the wall, a set of individual maps on an easel or stand, or a set of large map cards which you remove from an envelope and use like flash cards.

Use a chart when you want to reinforce visually what you and the class are saying. You may want to explain an idea you are presenting. Or you may plan to organize visually in some way what the class has said in brainstorming, and so you plan to chart members' responses on the chalkboard or on a large sheet of paper.

If you plan to deal with a topic which you will want to highlight visually, use a poster made of drawings or pictures. Whatever the chief mood, idea, or insight which you wish to suggest, select your pictures or make your drawings so as to convey this particular idea only. If you wish to include persuasive or explanatory Bible or life-related subject matter, prepare a chart for this purpose. Your poster may be simply some magazine pictures pasted to a large sheet of posterboard. Or, a newspaper picture with headlines may suggest vividly the idea you want members to get.

Pictures and objects.—You may come to the point in class Bible study where you are helping the class to understand Absalom's feelings and something of his motivations and personality. You have analyzed well the Scripture passages which interpret Absalom. The artist's portrayal of Absalom which you show for class analysis may come from an album of religious art, or it may be an individual drawing. But you may not be able to locate an actual painting portraying Absalom as the artist conceived him. If this is the case, find three or four good paintings of young men in their late twenties. Make sure that different personalities are portrayed. These paintings will heighten the mental and emotional involvement of class members as you use them to help members decide which one is "Absalom."

The object you use in teaching can come from almost anywhere. The more creative your imagination, the easier it is to find an object which will help you to illustrate—or focus members' attention upon—Bible truth. You may find a stone which has in it a deep hole caused by the constant, gradual dripping of water. Use this in an adult class to illustrate the possible effect upon Absalom's personality and character of the repeated sins of David. Or you may use this same approach to help young adults appreciate the condition out of which Absalom was obligated to escape with God's help. Other objects come easily to mind, such as an insect which eats its parents (use with young adults) or one which kills its young (use with older adults). You may choose, on the other hand, to find a rather complicated object to which you attach no particular significance for the coming Bible study. Plan, instead, to involve members in discovering their own significance in the object in light of the chief issue of the Bible passages.

Materials for written response.—Materials for securing written responses from class members take several forms. First there are the simple slips of paper and pencils with which you receive unsigned written reactions from members. Just cut two or three plain white sheets of paper into four, six, or eight strips. Then gather a handful of short pencils which have been discarded by others, and you are in business. After use, wrap a rubber band around the pencils, put them in your coat pocket or purse, and you are prepared for next time.

Surveys, checklists, or questionnaires make up the next most structured form of response-securing materials. A one-page elementary checklist or questionnaire often will serve your purpose, which usually will be to focus attention, stimulate discussion, and/or lay the foundation for careful analysis and discussion later in the session. You also may write your questions or points for checking on the chalkboard before class time. Cover with a cloth or newspaper fastened in the easiest way to the chalkboard frame. Prepare sheets of paper and pencils on which members can correctly relate their written responses by copying only the numbers of the questions on their papers. Later tabulation and discussion comes quite easily using these coded responses.

Tests, workbooks, and programed learning materials may need to be secured commercially. But you can make adaptations of these materials which may be all that you and the class desire. A good approach to preparing these is for you and one or two of your more creative class members to study forms which respected educators have prepared. Decide what features of these materials to adapt in order to aid in more thoughtful class Bible study. Then prepare your version of the test, workbook page, or programed learning sequence.

Classroom Arrangement

The chairs.—Place your chairs so that each class member can see the face of each other member. Serious, personally involving conversation or discussion rarely takes place between persons who are not looking one another in the eye. Class discussion of Bible truth and application is no exception to this principle. If your chairs for any reason prevent this ideal arrangement, come as close to this plan of seating as you can. Even seats which are locked together by fours or eights can be arranged so that members face each other. Single chairs can be placed around a section of a stationary pew. If you anticipate problems in securing the chair arrangement you desire, start to work on the situation a day or two in advance of the class session. A less fancy classroom with movable chairs will foster serious class Bible study more than the "choice" pews, row on row, in a larger area.

Moreover, you had better arrange the chairs yourself unless you know that the one doing it for you knows what you want. If you find that there simply is no way to prevent your class members from sitting row on row facing only you, do not despair. You still can use teaching procedures which bring members face to face and which help to overcome this hindrance to individual involvement in Bible study.

A table.—You need a medium-sized table at the front of your classroom. On this sturdy surface some four or five feet long, you will place books; your teaching notes, eraser, and chalk from time to time during the session; and other teaching aids. You may even lean against this table occasionally, or sit on the corner of it as you move in a relaxed manner toward one or the other of your class members who is responding. A desk or any other good substitute for a table will do, of course.

Checking with a Team Teacher

You may teach within a framework where two or more classes meet together for a short time before classes separate and engage in their own Bible study. Often this group or department period is thought of as preparing all class members for Bible study, along with accomplishing some other important purposes. Prior planning and understanding between you and the leader of this first period—your "team teacher"—is essential if you are to make Christ-honoring use of this opening session.

What matters do you two need to be together on? First, you want to know what he plans to do that will have a bearing on later class Bible study. Since this period helps to set the intellectual stage for the next session in small groups (classes), what he will do has an important bearing on how you will begin the class session. You want to know the content of his feature, where the film, role playing, case study, or newspaper clipping leaves the issue he is spotlighting, and so on. You also need to know the length of time this first session will last.

These matters of coordination often are clarified at a previous planning meeting. Sometimes you, the other teachers, and he work out together this opening period. Thus you know just where his contribution to the morning's Bible teaching will leave off and where yours will begin. When you and the leader of this first session are together on the purpose and nature of the period, you can clarify matters by telephone or mail or a quick personal conference.

This first period may be longer than we have been assuming, however, as in certain other forms of team teaching. The speaker in the first session may plan to bring an extended lecture on which you and other teachers later will guide class follow-up study. In this case, you will do well to secure a copy of his lecture, or at least an outline into which you may write his key facts and interpretations. Thus you will have opportunity to study and reflect in advance upon basic ideas which he will discuss.

Last-Minute Checkup

When is the "last minute," practically speaking? When do you make that last checkup before class time? Perhaps the last minute, as far as your preparation for teaching is concerned, is that latest time when you still can do something satisfactory about insuring the teaching situation which you have planned for the session. After this time, if something goes wrong you improvise with the Spirit's continued help.

Check your teaching plan carefully, perhaps the night before, or a few hours before class time. Make sure that equipment is ready for everything you plan to do. Spot even the chalk and eraser as you arrive a little early. Someone may have borrowed yours after you placed them in the chalkboard tray yesterday, and forgot to bring them back. Also as you look over your teaching plan the last time, consider the time element again. Do you still feel that you will have time for all that you have planned? Does each procedure still have that ring of genuineness and stimulation for you which it had when, deeply involved in creative planning, you mapped it out?

Remain alert to the news. Have events just occurred in the community or nation which simply must be used to help form the framework of this Bible study? Would ignoring them make the Bible study you lead seem to verge on the irrelevant? Or must you recognize new factors in order to give spiritual balance to the study you had planned to lead? By all means insert these new experiences into your teaching plan and allow God's Word to speak to the literal here and now. A new spiritual significance will come into the Bible study experience which your class engages in.

Check up as late as possible on special assignments. Call your key class member or resource person on Sunday morning. Make sure his alarm went off! Is the leader of the opening period all set to do what you two agreed upon? Thus you still can plan to begin the class session as you have discussed it. And telephone the custodian to see if the screen is ready, the extension cord on hand. Was he able to get the room warm, or the air-conditioning working? Did he find the chalk and eraser?

Unbelievable as it may seem, the best teaching plans have come to grief through not making a last-minute check of such elementary details as these just mentioned.

3
Introducing New Approaches

Chapter 2 introduced four basic teaching methods. Beginning with chapter 4, we will look at ways that you can carry out such methods in your class. First, however, we need to look at some other valuable methods for teaching. This chapter will describe ten of these—each of which has a place in group Bible study. Later chapters will give you help in using these in the teaching plan that you develop for a particular session.

Assignment-Report Forum

Teaching through this approach, you and the class make an assignment to one or more class members which requires work *outside of class*. This activity, of course, must be related to Bible study. It may require (1) study; (2) reflection; (3) interview; (4) experiment or other project in Christian living; or (5) workbook, programed learning, or other similar activity. Class members carry out the assignment and report their findings, feelings, and other interpretations of their experiences. You and the rest of the class react to the reports in terms of their significance for major issues in the unit of Bible study under consideration.

Case-Study Forum

This classroom procedure is a basic teaching approach, even though it obviously must be implemented by such other methods as lecture, informal discussion, or small group study. You may use any one of several ways to present the case study to the class. You simply may tell the facts (lecture). Or you may use a film or filmstrip, a written statement of the case for each member, a recording, and so on.

The case may come from the actual experience of someone in the age range of your class, from literature, from history, or elsewhere.

The situation involved relates both to the central truth of the Bible passages being studied and to class members' spiritual concerns. Usually you include an unsolved problem in the statement of facts which goes to the heart of the Bible truth involved. You use this case as the framework upon which the entire Bible study period is based.[1] A chief advantage of this teaching approach is that you often can help members with serious spiritual problems without the risk of alienating them by being too personal.

Small-Group Study Forum

To use the small-group study forum, divide the class into two or more parts. This is to help members give close attention to selected aspects of the Bible material or its implications. Each group usually chooses a discussion leader to keep the group study moving and later to report to you and the class. After six or eight minutes of small-group study, call the groups back to the larger circle, ask for reports, and invite general class reactions. Then build upon this discussion as you continue the Bible study through lecture and, possibly, informal discussion.

The Bible-related subjects which you ask the small groups to study can vary widely, of course. You may ask them to search the Scripture passage for certain statements, or to agree upon what certain verses mean. You may ask them to evaluate certain teachings in the passage, or otherwise analyze the biblical content. Or you may ask the groups to agree upon what class members can do in response to the clear teaching of God's Word.

Drama Forum

You may use drama as a basic teaching approach even though you will lecture, ask questions, and so on, as supplementary procedures. Several forms of drama help achieve stimulating Bible study. With *role playing* you lead members in a spontaneous, impromptu acting out of a spiritual problem situation, often involving a conflict in human relationships. Then you and the class analyze the feelings and attitudes portrayed and relate this experience to your present point in Bible study.[2]

---

[1] See, also, Wesner Fallaw, *The Case Method in Pastoral and Lay Education* (Philadelphia: The Westminster Press, 1963), pp. 197–200.

[2] See, also, Alan F. Klein, *How to Use Role Playing Effectively* (New York: Association Press, 1959), pp. 9–11, 40–53.

Interpretive Scripture reading is a teaching process where you ask one or more members to interpret Bible persons or situations in a given passage. Members use either exact Bible wordage or interpret in their own words. You may follow this type of dramatic Bible reading with class analysis of the interpretations given.

The *skit* is a simple playlet approach which you use to highlight a biblical situation, spiritual problem, or other life relationship which is important to members' gaining depth of insight into Bible truth. At least a small amount of rehearsal is done.

Debate Forum

When teaching with debate forum, ask two or four members in advance to study opposite sides of some biblical question or issue vitally related to the achievement of your teaching aim. The statement for debate might read something like this: "*Resolved:* That a young adult's only hope of achieving his real selfhood is to make a complete break with his parents." No doubt you recognize this teaching idea as one which goes far into some of the spiritual issues involved in the biblical study of Absalom and David. You might use lecture to introduce the Bible study, then call for the debate. Each affirmative and negative speaker speaks only once, talking some two or three minutes apiece. The "rebuttal" phase of the brief debate takes the form of other class members' reactions.

Lead members to determine where truth was expressed on *both* sides. You and the class also evaluate biblical passages used in the debate and note relevant verses omitted. Summation of the best thoughts expressed during the session may relate closely to the achieving of your teaching aim.

Test Forum

The reason that test forum qualifies as a basic Bible teaching approach is that when your questions are well phrased, you take the whole class period agreeing upon the answers in light of the Bible passage being studied. With proper advance understanding and agreement of the class, you ask members to take the written test based on important aspects of the passage for study. Members may sign their papers or not, as they wish. Unsigned may be better as a rule. Then you may collect the papers, mix them up, and redistribute them for reading aloud and "grading." Or you may read all the answers yourself. The rest of the session is spent discussing the best answers to the questions, in light of the passages under study.

Team-Teaching Forum

You may approach this teaching procedure in one of several ways. You may invite one or more persons to help plan and evaluate the study and to assist you in teaching. Each person may take a specific phase of the topic or Bible content to speak upon. If all of you address the class one after the other before the class reacts, the procedure takes on the nature of a *symposium*. If you address comments and questions to one another before class reaction, you are using something of a *panel* approach. Or one teacher may address two or more classes, dealing with foundation or background Bible content and concepts.

Then classes go to separate places for follow-up discussion. You and your members discuss specific questions which the first presentation has raised. You add additional biblical information and insights, and lead your class to interpret and apply Bible meanings. In this second phase of the study, you yourself may use lecture, informal discussion, or other procedures to accomplish your teaching aim.

Another type of shared or team teaching involves your inviting someone in to become a silent partner in teaching. This person helps plan, listens, observes, and reacts later in the class session for everyone's benefit, or privately to you concerning what took place during the study.

Colloquy

Teaching through the colloquy involves some of the same procedures as does use of small-group study and the panel (team teaching) forum just discussed. You would use this approach with a class at least as large as twelve members. Otherwise the procedures might crush the individuals!

First, assign three or four members the task of becoming informed as well as possible about the meaning, implications, and/or follow-through responses which the Bible passages involve. These are your resource persons. (The resource persons also may be team teachers from outside the class.) Divide the rest of the class into two or more groups. Members of each group choose a discussion leader–spokesman. Then they phrase from their *advance study* the two or three most significant questions which they feel are involved in the Bible content. These questions may relate to Bible facts, but probably will deal with meaning and use in life relationships. After six or eight minutes of small-group discussion, spokesmen from the small groups come with their questions to the front of the room and sit as a panel half-facing the resource persons and the rest of the class. You serve as discussion moderator, of course.

First one small group spokesman and then another puts a question to the panel of resource persons. The panel of spokesmen and the panel of resource persons first seek the best answer to each question. Then you and the rest of the class come in on the discussion. When the first question is answered by this process to the satisfaction of all (or most), move to the next question.

Watch the time and lead in summarizing some five minutes before the end of the period. If you sense that the number of questions is large, you may want to lead the two panels in arranging the questions in a spiritually profitable order before panel discussion begins. This order of questions should lead class study to the achievement of your teaching aim before the session is over.

Audio-Visual Forum

This teaching approach involves use of tape and disc recordings, films, television, filmstrips, slides, or other similar teaching aids. Through this means you lay the foundation for Bible analysis, interpretation, and application leading to the achieving of your teaching aim. Through lecture you set the intellectual stage for the audio-visual. You perhaps appoint a reaction group (listening team). Then you present the audio-visual. The remainder of the class period is devoted to concentrated Bible study, building upon this first phase of the session, upon responses of your reaction team, upon other class members' insights, and upon your own contributions.

Book Review Forum

This Bible-teaching approach is listed here rather than being included under assignment-report forum. The reason for this is that in some instances you and the class may be studying not only a book or portion of the Bible but also a book interpreting a book or part of the Bible. In other words, in helping the class to study the relationship between Absalom and David, you have decided to base your teaching on a well written book, play, or other writing dealing with this tragic son-father relationship. The selected Bible passages still are your main textbook. In this procedure you use the lecture approach primarily, unless you want to vary lecture with other approaches such as assignment-report, small-group reaction, reaction groups, thought-provoking questions, and so on.

Supplementary Approaches in Bible Teaching

We have said that some Bible-teaching approaches seem best used to supplement or support more basic procedures. We have also acknowledged that you conceivably can abbreviate the basic approaches and use them as supporting methods of teaching. In like manner, you possibly can expand some of the supplementary procedures which we are about to consider, and base a whole session of Bible study upon them. All of these teaching approaches are offered here to be used as the Holy Spirit leads you to use them best.

Group conversation.—Use this class study process as you begin the session. Indeed, you may use it as you begin a new class group. For this procedure is one to help your members get acquainted and establish a communicating relationship with one another. Arrange chairs in a circle so that members can face one another, if possible. As you begin the session, lead the class in talking about some experience from early life which everyone probably has shared in. When possible, you choose this topic of informal conversation so that it can have implications for the Bible study to follow and for the achieving of your teaching aim. Seek to engage every member in some way in the conversation, trying to secure nods and smiles if nothing else. When members are talking with you and with one another, move into more direct Bible study.[3]

Brainstorming.—Brainstorming is one of the most valuable teaching procedures you can use. For it is here that you invite members to react most creatively and honestly to important yet difficult implications in the Bible passage. You may call for these free, spontaneous responses at any stage of the study. You call for the immediate thinking and feeling of members upon some problem or question important for achieving your teaching aim. As members

[3] See, also, Rachel D. Dubois and Mew Soong Li, *The Art of Group Conversation* (New York: Association Press, 1963), pp. 19 ff.

respond, write their statements *without questioning* on the chalkboard. When all responses have been accepted without criticism and written down, lead the class then to analyze, organize, perhaps refine, the ideas, and get them into a form which will best aid further Bible study.

Circular response.—When you use circular response in teaching, you call for individual responses to a problem, as in brainstorming. But the response situation is more structured. Before class time arrange chairs in something of a circle. Then at the desired point in class study, ask a thought-provoking question to which everyone can have some relevant response if he wishes. To encourage response, use something of a game approach by asking one member to start class response, the one beside him to react next, and so on around the circle. No one is to be left out. You add genuineness and purposefulness to the responses by jotting key words of each response on the chalkboard for use later in class discussion.

Written survey of the class.—Ask the class to participate in a written poll or survey. Usually the responses are unsigned. The survey may be a questionnaire, an opinionnaire, or other form of reaction sheet. First, members write their responses to a biblically based question from you which is important to the achieving of your teaching aim. Then collect the papers and either read responses aloud or list them on the chalkboard. You may tabulate or otherwise analyze the responses, or merely refer appropriately to them as Bible study continues, depending upon your teaching plan.

Reaction group.—Before you begin lecturing or hearing statements from others concerning the Bible passage, appoint two or more persons to listen carefully and react to what is said. One may listen for statements which need clarifying. Another may listen and react later to what he agreed with. Still another may react to what he mildly or strongly disagreed with. Call for these reactions after your lecture or other teaching procedure. Invite other class members to discuss each reaction. Of course, you as teacher should lead in clarifying and in otherwise meeting Bible study needs during this time. Sometimes this procedure can take almost all the study time unless you purposely plan the session differently.

Picture study.—At some point in the class Bible study, place or unveil before the class a picture with religious significance. The picture may portray a biblical scene, or it may show or suggest biblical or spiritual meanings. Ask members to study the picture silently from some clearly stated point of view. You may ask them to discover Bible knowledge, to interpret the feelings of biblical characters, to identify biblical truth in the scene, to express what spiritual meanings they see in the picture, and so on. Then use the responses in moving more deeply into study of the Bible passage.

Reflection-response.—Often the time arrives during the class session when you want members to reflect seriously and silently upon some biblical truth or implication. State the question or other spiritual problem and allow members a minute or two in which to reflect upon it. Then call upon members to share with the class what they think and feel about the matter. You may ask the class to read, reflect, and respond concerning a Bible passage. Or the reflection may be upon your interpretation of the passage, upon someone else's interpretation which seems to pose a problem for Christian believers, and so on.

Testimony.—Some Bible teaching aims call for a place in the teaching plan for an appropriate class member to give a testimony. Perhaps, for example, you are helping the class to accept for themselves the value of a great Bible truth. At the right place in class discussion you ask a member, whom you know well and have possibly contacted beforehand, if he will tell the class what this Bible truth has meant to him and why he relies upon it. You then use his testimony as you continue with class study.

Reflection-prayer.—This classroom procedure differs from reflection-response. Use it when you do not expect to call for verbal response—when you want members instead to pause during class discussion, reflect upon what has just been said, and sincerely pray about it as it relates to Christ's will, their own understanding and attitudes, and their response to God's Word. After the class has engaged in reflection and prayer, continue according to your teaching plan or conclude the class session.

Introducing New Bible Study Approaches

In a short time we shall be considering in more detail several ways of leading dynamic Bible study. Let us pause here briefly to anticipate a feeling you may have as you see what is involved in helping your class to think through and respond to God's Word. You may feel that your class would not relate well to teaching procedures so mentally and emotionally strenuous and perhaps so different from what they have been used to. Moreover, you may feel deeply self-conscious about suddenly breaking out in class with teaching procedures like these. So you may hesitate even to attempt what seem to be difficult ways of leading Bible study.

Even if you do want to try using these more stimulating approaches, you still may wonder seriously how you ever will accomplish this change successfully. And so pause here to consider briefly just how you will go about introducing to the class new ways of Bible study. Having these ideas and guidelines in mind, you can come with greater confidence to the detailed discussion of new teaching procedures.

What is the attitude of your class toward trying stimulating new experiences? You may be teaching a class of youth or young adults —or older adults!—who would welcome warmly the new ways of Bible study which you might introduce to them. They even may have asked you for this change. Or they may have talked to one another— and you heard of it—about wanting more stimulating Bible study experiences. And so, perhaps at a class meeting during the week or even at your regular meeting time—you make the grand announcement! Beginning the next class session, you are going to try some new approaches to Bible study.

Of course, the beginning of a new teaching year is also a good time to declare your resolve to a class of wide-awake members. And even with a class of adults who do not welcome change so much, the new teaching year is a good time to state your desire to seek better ways, with their prayers and help.

Be Casual

You may not feel that a sudden change from continual lecture to thoughtful class Bible study will achieve the best results. And so you want to find a better way of transforming your Bible teaching. You do not have to make the grand announcement, or wait until a new teaching year begins, or delay until the first Sunday in January. You can begin at the very next class session to enrich and deepen the quality of your teaching. And you can make this change in your teaching without dramatically calling attention to what is happening. Just be casual.

Being casual is a mood as much as it is a method for bringing about change. You begin to do new things in your teaching as if they were just a natural part of what you always have done. If you have never done these things before, do them now in such a related, quiet way that class members respond in this same natural way.

For instance, what if your usual method of teaching is lecture from beginning to end? What can you do in order to move quietly into more thought-provoking Bible study experiences for your class members?

You can combine *reflection-response* with lecture. Somewhere early in your lecture about Absalom's relationship with his father David, ask class members what they feel were some factors which helped to pull Absalom away from David early in the young man's life. The point here is that you have stopped talking and quite naturally have asked your class members to bring their minds seriously to bear upon the situation you are discussing. And you have done this so casually that your members are more likely to respond thoughtfully to your question than they are to note wonderingly that you are letting them have a part in the class Bible study experience.

Another quite natural way to move out of just lecturing is to combine lecture with *brainstorming*. Your approach is similar, of course, to that in combining lecture with reflection-response. At the point in your lecture, say, where you want members to think hard about Absalom's decision to rebel against his father, pose a problem to the class. You may pause quite casually and say something like this: *By the way, just what combinations of choices did Absalom actually have here? You young people are better able to suggest possibilities than I am.*

Combining lecture with *testimony* also is a very natural and quiet way to start bringing members' thoughts and feelings into class discussion. You may be teaching older adults and have come to the place where David grieved aloud over the death of Absalom. Here you pause and ask a man if he is willing to help the class understand something of David's feelings by telling a little about the loss of his own son. Or, this early in your transition from pure lecturing, it might be better to help a class member, whom you know will not be offended, to begin his story and let him confirm and finish it. This person probably should be one whom you earlier have heard tell about his son's death.

On the other hand, suppose that you already have begun to use, say, informal discussion in your teaching; that is, leading class Bible study through the use of carefully phrased questions. Yet you notice that only a few class members respond to the questions. You want to use some teaching procedures which will involve the whole class in reflection and response. You casually say after perhaps the second or third question (or when the right question for this comes along): *Now since opinions on this question vary so much, let's start here with John and go around the room hearing from everyone before we start reacting to what different ones of you are saying.* Thus you have brought *circular response* into your teaching approach to reinforce the already stimulating informal discussion procedure.

In a similar way you can move without fanfare from *individual classroom research-report* to *small-group research-report,* simply by pointing out in a casual way that the particular passage under consideration is best examined by three or four persons thinking it through together at this point rather than just one person's looking at it. The teaching manner being sought here is that of introducing new classroom procedures so quietly and naturally that members feel the appropriateness of what you are doing and do not resist.

Be Gradual

Being gradual in changing your way of teaching may sound like the same guideline as being casual, but there is enough difference in concept to discuss them separately. In fact, you may be teaching a class which is so alert, progressive, and purposeful that you do not need to be casual. But you feel that, in order for your teaching approaches to be effective, you should move slowly from one type of procedure to a closely related one. Being casual thus refers chiefly to your manner in using new teaching approaches. Being gradual refers to the sequence of methods which you use in leading the class to new ways of Bible study.

We already have referred to the naturalness of pausing in your lecturing to call for the kinds of responses which your class members are sure to be able to make—if they have been listening. Thus you already may have used in class a simple *question-and-answer* process in focusing members' minds upon what you have been saying. For instance, you may ask: *Now, again, what was Absalom doing at this stage to stir up rebellion against David?* Here you simply help members to catch up with you on the Bible facts you have been giving.

But in this session you move to *brainstorming,* a gradual but important transition to more thoughtful class activity. Here you ask a different kind of question: *By the way, just what combinations of choices did Absalom have just before he led the rebellion against David?* Thus members are led to use Bible facts plus their own feelings and creative imagination.

In the next session you use *circular response* to aid every class member in opening up and becoming a part of the Bible study. Perhaps you use a question similar to the one you used in brainstorming. The fourth stage in stimulating class thought and response may come as you use the slightly more structured *unsigned written responses.* You see that this procedure goes a little beyond brainstorming and circular response. And your question here may be a little more personal. If you are teaching older adults, your question might be: *Summing it all up, what can you say in defense of Absalom's action?* If you are helping young adults to think through this son-father situation, your question for written unsigned response might be: *Summing it all up, what can you say in disapproving of Absalom's action?*

These four teaching procedures move gradually from one level of intellectual and emotional involvement to another. All things being equal, this procedure seems to be the best way to introduce new Bible study approaches to the class. Similar transitions may be made from testimony to assignment report, from informal discussion and individual classroom research-report to small-group research-report, from team-teaching (panel) forum to debate forum to colloquy, from informal discussion to formal discussion, and so on.

Be Genuine

As you prayerfully decide upon what teaching procedures to use in the next class session, your spiritual motivations are of the highest. You are trying to determine those ways of leading class Bible study which will help your members to face up in the most sincere way possible to the meaning of God's Word. Therefore, your teaching methods are not gimmicks, tricks, ways of manipulating, methods without spirituality and compassion.

Use these teaching procedures in the most realistic, genuine way you can. Cause your class members to feel needed, respected, and loved through the ways you teach. When you use *brainstorming,* write all responses on the chalkboard. Give each contribution full acceptance. Make sure that these responses become a basic part of class discussion. When you use *role playing,* make sure that interpretations are accepted fully, understood clearly, and related accurately to the Bible applications being studied. When you use *formal discussion,* keep your teaching aim and spiritual purposes in mind. Do not get tangled up in procedure so as to become mechanical and superficial. The group processes which we are considering are revealed to Christians by the Holy Spirit in order for them to achieve *reality* and *purposefulness* in Bible study. Make sure that you use your teaching methods in a way to achieve these results.

Be Thorough

The success of your decision to introduce more thought-provoking, dynamic Bible study in your class will depend partly upon the thoroughness with which you prepare and with which you carry out your plans. Consider the time factor. Group study processes require plenty of *time* if the experience is to be genuine and deep. This does not mean that more than your usual thirty or forty-five minutes is essential for anything of value to be done. But it does mean that you consider carefully just how long certain procedures will take, and plan accordingly. It does mean that you note the time factor before you start teaching, that you be ready to revise your teaching plan if the time should be short, that you think through carefully how to end the session if your time schedule should go awry for one good reason or another.

Organizing and preparing *teaching supplies* also requires thoroughness. Brainstorming falls far short of its potential if chalkboard, chalk, and eraser are not ready for use. Class members will think less of this teaching procedure if you are not equipped to handle it so as to reap the full benefit of its nature as a learning process. The *unsigned survey of the class* falls flat as a member-involving procedure if you come just one short of having enough pencils for everyone. You have excluded this person from participating. It is better not to use the written response approach if you have not made sure that all can join in.

Then comes the matter of thoroughness in *handling the procedure.* Allow your members to receive the full impact of the procedure's potential. When you use *role playing,* take pains to do it right. Don't try to use shortcuts. Plan carefully all the steps, gauge the time needed, and give the time needed. Choose the problem situation so wisely that you are on the point of achieving your teaching aim all the time.

As you use *reflection-response,* make it clear what members are to reflect upon. One group member once broke the silence in a very loosely handled situation and pleaded, "I don't even know what I am supposed to be thinking about!" Allow plenty of time for reflection. Do you realize how long two minutes are in class reflection time? It will seem like an eternity to you unless you remember that genuine reflection takes more than thirty seconds. And call for responses from everyone if members expect this. The procedure is defeated if members reflect and then do not have the chance to share what the Spirit has put on their hearts to say. The class will not want to use such an insincere process again.

The very genius of these group study processes is that they provide time for members to become involved mentally and emotionally with Bible truth and its implications. Whether you use picture study, colloquy, team teaching, or other approaches, take time to help class members probe deeply for spiritual insights. Allow the procedure to run its course, every step in a manner satisfying to the class. Thus you will find members coming eagerly to new ways of Bible analysis and interpretation. Your job will become holding them back, if anything; guiding the direction of their participation; insuring fair play in discussion time; keeping class Bible study purposeful.

4
Varying the Lecture

Lecture may be the teaching method which you have used almost exclusively in the past. Because of its value and also its shortcomings, we shall consider it more fully here than otherwise we might do. And we shall go further and see what happens for you and your class members when you transform lecture into lecture forum.[1]

Just as it is hard to imagine any stimulating teaching which does not provide, sooner or later, for reaction from your class members, so it is difficult to imagine any constructive, enriching teaching which does not involve lecture. Lecturing is speaking to the class in a (usually) planned, more or less formal manner as you present Bible facts and interpretations to class members for their reflection and response. With all teaching methods, there are times when you need to *tell* members something, to inform them, to prepare them intellectually or emotionally, to set the intellectual stage for class thought and reaction, to summarize. Your members desire informed comments about the passages of Scripture which they are studying. You are usually the one to give this interpretation to them. Thus you will see in this book that you use lecture every time you teach, even if it is for only short spans of time on each occasion.

Circumstances occasionally may justify your using all the class time talking to your members. Time for the study may have become suddenly very short. Or maybe the unit of study that you and the class have begun seems clearly to require this one-way communication during the first, introductory session. There are many biblical facts, customs, and relationships during the time of David and Absalom, for instance, which you and the class need to have before you prior to further study of, say, a five-session unit. So you may have consulted

[1] See, also, Findley B. Edge, *Helping the Teacher* (Nashville: Broadman Press, 1959), pp. 104–10.

with key class members and they agree that you should take all the time in the first session, lecturing. They will make their active contributions to class study later! Or if you have not secured some class acceptance for doing all the talking during this first session of the unit, you might begin by explaining your procedure with consideration and reasonableness. Your class readily will accept your decision without feeling that you simply want only your opinions to be expressed.

You can use this same approach when the Bible passages are especially complicated. This procedure in such a case assumes that you have a later session in which you and members can come to grips with meanings and implications of the passages.

Last to be mentioned here is that rare time when you feel that the Bible passages and topic are so sensitive for the situation prevailing that you had better "keep talking" the whole class period. Maybe members are not ready spiritually to start expressing themselves. The church or community situation may be so critical at this time that you know God's Word needs to be expressed, but not man's recriminations and misunderstandings. It is true that sooner or later your class members will need to react to you and to one another about what God's Word means to them in the situation. But this particular class session may not be that time.

Your own Spirit-guided judgment will tell you what are those other infrequent times when you will decide that you had better lecture the whole period without allowing time for class discussion. But these times probably will be widely spaced over the year.

Lecture Forum

You may use lecture forum in many forms as you lead Bible study. But even some of these approaches to varying the lecture may leave class members so uninvolved and cold that you might as well have just lectured and not made any gestures toward allowing members to respond. Yet there are ways to use lecture forum which prove so stimulating that the only thing lacking in the session is time. Here are some of the possibilities.

Look first at just about the most unpromising use of lecture forum that you can make. We shall call it the "Any questions?" approach. Of course, this effort by you to enlist class thought and reaction to what the Bible says is better than none. And the mood and manner in which you ask for questions can have a lot to do with the success you achieve. Moreover, you may have in your class one or two persons who *just will* say what is on their minds and hearts about the passages you have discussed. So, in spite of yourself, you may see a pretty good discussion develop as some members exchange convictions and try to come to grips with what you have said, and with the meaning of God's Word for their lives.

On the other hand, haven't you been in group study situations when the speaker finished and asked, "Any questions?" and no one said a word? Why didn't anyone ask a question? Of course, the time for the period may have run out, and no one wanted to start anything that would make the class late adjourning. But at other times, class members may have been shy. Or the lecture may have dealt with controversial matters and no one wanted to be first to react or to comment voluntarily one way or the other. Or the speaker may have been so dogmatic that no one dared express a different view, and he had said all that there was to be said on one side of the topic! Or his comments may have been so technical and highly informed on Bible lore that no one dared try to add—or take away—anything. In situations like these, your "Any questions?" often will not get any questions, or any other type of response except stony silence.

Perhaps a surer way of securing response from class members after you have lectured is to ask specific questions. At least you are one step nearer to teacher-class interaction, for you provide the questions rather than ask for them. Class members can come up with answers or other comments, and not try to phrase more difficult "right questions" to ask. And sometimes members are more ready to offer answers than to bring up hard, confronting questions.

What kind of questions will you ask? Questions similar to those suggested for use in teaching through informal discussion (chap. 5) support well the lecture approach.

You can stimulate class thought on, and evaluation of, your biblical interpretations in other ways besides just asking questions. Notice these ways of developing the forum part of the lecture forum approach. All of them involve your securing reflective reaction from class members. You want to know if they have heard what you said, have understood it, and if they have a value judgment concerning your comments and the Bible statements themselves.

The following procedures can help you to call forth these responses. *Small-group discussion* of your lecture can become highly profitable. Discussion questions such as the ones suggested for use in informal discussion guide the small-group conversations well. Or you may *arrange before class time* with certain members to play the friendly, well-intentioned role of *"hard-to-convince" questioners.* After lecturing for some ten or fifteen minutes, these "assistant teachers" of yours speak out one by one and "spontaneously," using questions such as we have discussed. Or you and these selected members may agree upon questions much more suitable for your class's needs at this time.

Alternatively, before you lecture you may *appoint three or four members to listen carefully* to what you say and be prepared to ask for clarifications, to agree with you at important points, and to disagree in a friendly manner with your facts or interpretations at certain other points. After you lecture about a third of the time, ask these reactors to lead off in digging into the biblical truths expounded by you, what the Bible says, what members think, and so on.

Thus you see that lecture forum can become one of the most honest, stimulating ways of leading your class in Bible study. Now let us consider a specific way to achieve our teaching aim using lecture forum.

We are ready to put ourselves into the actual teaching situation where we are leading Bible study through the use of lecture forum. We are using teaching aim IV that we developed in chapter 1: *To help class members decide upon ways by which they will seek to deepen the bonds of respect and affection between themselves and their parents.*

Beginning the Study

You are using a relatively "low temperature" teaching method as you begin to teach through lecture forum. Therefore, use a "high temperature" way of involving class members mentally and emotionally in the study of these Bible passages. Perhaps the experiences which took place in the preclass period aroused members and focused their attention keenly upon a chief issue in this study. If such an experience did not occur, yet this first session did relate to your Bible study topic, you need to provide the "sparks" which will heighten interest in the study. You might take friendly issue with some interpretation which was made in the first period. Stir up a little pro-and-con discussion over some situation described in the assembly.

Or, if you are not relating to the preclass session, present a news item or other statement which arouses the emotions of class members. Read to the class a brief article or editorial statement which says something like, "The nation is crumbling because America's youth have lost all respect for their parents!" The more provocative the reference, the better. Encourage just enough discussion to generate warm feelings and set the stage for interested Bible study.

Then show briefly how this topic relates to what has just been said and how it grows out of the Bible studies which have preceded this one. If your class members value this type of learning aid, use a chart spotlighting this topic in relationship to previous ones in the unit.[2] But go right into your lecture while members still possess that emotional involvement in the life situation to which the Bible passages will speak.

After you have spoken a few sentences to explain the setting for this Bible study, pause to appoint some *reaction groups*. This is one of the ways by which you will encourage members to listen and to evaluate what you will be saying. Their later reaction to your statements will tell you much more clearly that you reached them today than will a friendly "Good message this morning, teacher."

If you have ten or more members in your class, appoint three reaction groups of two persons each. If you have only five or six members, you may simply appoint three persons in order to leave the others free to make other contributions in the forum period. Ask Group 1 to listen carefully to what you soon will be saying about the Bible passages and note *what happens to Absalom* in the course of the story. Group 2 will note *David's lost opportunities* to establish a better relationship with Absalom. Group 3 will listen and be prepared to react later as to *Absalom's lost opportunities* to draw closer to his father.

You can see the purposefulness with which these members will be listening to your exposition. And other class members will find it all but impossible not to watch, also, for the main spiritual threads which you have pointed out. They will want to satisfy themselves about

---

[2] See Ford, *op. cit.*, pp. 15 ff.

these questions and also check on the observation powers of their fellow class members.

You may have some reason to feel that you should not attempt these specifically structured reaction groups at this stage in your teaching. If this is true, you can achieve something of the value of this procedure anyway. Simply alert the whole class to the fact that you will attempt to help them see these three developments in the Bible story which have just been suggested for the reaction groups. Explain that the final part of class study will depend upon a clear awareness of these three ideas.

Going Further in Bible Study

Now take up your lecturing again. Explain briefly Absalom's parentage, his likely childhood experiences in David's unpromising household, the half-brother troubles, murder, flight to the north, return but exclusion from home, jealousy, apprehension, plotting, and so on. At the most appropriate place in your lecture, pause and call for the *testimony* which you have carefully arranged. Ask a member to tell the class about a time when he knew that his father was going to give a brother or sister something that he wanted very much. He will tell how he found out about his father's plan, how he felt, what he did, and so on. Perhaps a good time for this testimony is where you are telling about Absalom's discovery that Solomon, and not he, might inherit the throne.

Tie in closely with the feelings related in the testimony as you continue your lecture and bring the account on to Absalom's death and David's deep grief. You have planned your time, and knew that not over fifteen minutes would be needed for your lecture period. As you lectured, moreover, you *used the Bible* in part for your notes and encouraged class members to verify your points in their own Bibles as you stated chapter and verse for important interpretations.

Now ask the first reaction group to say what they discovered from your lecture. If time allows, an excellent procedure at this point is to give each of the three reaction groups about five minutes in which to talk over what each group member has perceived from the Bible study thus far in answer to the group's question. Lead other class members to get together and agree upon brief answers to all three questions. But if time is short, ask reaction group members individually to give their conclusions. After each pair has given its interpretations, encourage other class members to *use their Bibles* and either verify or challenge what the two members have just said. Lead the class finally to some agreement on these points.

Concluding the Study

You now have about five or ten minutes before the end of the class session. Begin to focus members' minds and hearts upon themselves and their parents. Use *circular response* as you pose a spiritual problem like this: What can a son [or daughter] do to develop more feeling of respect for parents? If the class is seated in something of a circle, start with a member who likely will make a serious, helpful response. Then, go to the one beside him, finally asking each one around the circle to suggest a possible answer. If members are seated row on row, you still seek the responses of all, going from one member to the next. As each person answers, determine the key word or phrase in his idea and list it on the chalkboard. As time allows, lead the class to suggest an order in which to do the things listed on the chalkboard that will offer spiritual development, inner satisfaction, and outward action.

With two or three minutes remaining, use *reflection-prayer* as you help the class to face the reality of their own actions. Ask members each to consider prayerfully his own answer to the question, What will I do this week to cause my parent who needs this most to know that I respect him? While members still are in silent prayer, and after at least a full minute of reflection, lead the class in prayer for Christ's guidance and power.

Team-Teaching Forum

Several forms of team or shared teaching provide opportunities for stimulating Bible study through variations of the lecture. The approach we are using here involves one person who perhaps uses fifteen or twenty minutes of lecture to lay a biblical foundation for later class analysis and reflection. This resource person may take what we have been calling the preclass or large-group session, or department period, for his specialized teaching. Then your class and other classes making up the larger group move to smaller rooms where they engage in further study under the leadership of the class teacher. Thus you and the first teacher, who has helped plan and will help evaluate, become a team in guiding Bible study. Teaching aim I is achieved well through this study approach: *To help class members examine the experiences of Absalom and David in their relationship as son and father.*

Beginning the Study

You as class teacher, together with your team teacher, have helped your members prepare for the team-teaching approach to Bible study. Perhaps in the last session you introduced this plan of study. You appointed, say, two *reaction groups* for this first session of team teaching. These groups need not ever involve the whole class. Out of a class of ten members in attendance, four persons or less in each reaction group are enough.

You asked the members of Group 1 each to listen to the lecturer and write down what seem to be the three most significant events which the lecturer mentions as he describes the history of Absalom and David. Members of Group 2 were to come to this session prepared to phrase two questions apiece regarding important gaps which the lecturer seems to leave in the story, or concerning important points of Bible information needing clarification.

Appointing these reaction groups at the close of the previous class session serves also to heighten the interest of other class members. They realize that they also may want to listen with mental alertness to the lecturer's account of Absalom and David, in order to participate intelligently in the subsequent class discussion. But you may have enlisted these reaction groups by mail, by telephone, in person at work, or in a recent class planning meeting.

The first member of your teaching team now lays the biblical foundation for later class study of the facts concerning Absalom and David. He secures mental and emotional involvement in the topic. He uses a chart or other means to show the relationship of this first topic to other studies in the unit. Then he presents a historical treatment of the life experiences which Absalom and David shared. He is aware of your knowledge-teaching aim, and so he confines himself to Bible facts and background. If you use team teaching again during this unit of Bible study, he will have opportunity then to join with you in helping members to gain understandings, appreciations, convictions, and plans for action in everyday living.

Going Further in Bible Study

Now you and the class move from this first period of Bible study into your own class session. Sometimes this regrouping is done simply, that is, the class stays in the same room and moves from large group study into small group, intensive study. But in our framework of discussion, the group will now move to a classroom and follow up on the background Bible study which the team teacher has offered.

As soon as members are settled, *divide the class* into two groups. Make sure that two members of each reaction group are in each of these small groups. These will serve as resource persons when small-group study begins. Ask each group to select a discussion leader who is not already one of the reaction group members. Resource persons usually don't render their best service to the group if they serve also as moderator of the group's discussion. And you want more class members, not fewer, to become involved.

Assign these three tasks to each group: (1) Based entirely on what you heard in the first period, and not using the Bible or other printed sources, list every separate event in the Absalom-David relationship and number these events in chronological order. (2) Agree on five events which occurred in the Absalom-David story that may have exerted the most influence on the tragic outcome of this son-father relationship. (3) Phrase three questions which point out important gaps in Bible information which remain after the lecture, or questions which ask for essential explanations of the lecturer's statements.

Allow the two groups about fifteen minutes in which to work out their answers. Circulate around and render any brief, quiet assistance that is needed.

Now regroup the class in a circle and ask discussion leaders to report. Prepare to record group answers on the chalkboard or discussion board. If you use the chalkboard, head the first column on the left side "Events." Then ask the leader of Group 1 to read in chronological order his list of events in the Absalom-David story. Write these one under the other on the chalkboard. If you use a discussion board, write key words in each event on a 4 by 6 card. Place these cards in the top holders on the board, in the group's suggested sequence. One advantage of the discussion board is that the cards may be saved easily and used for visual and other reference later in the unit.

After recording Group 1's list of historical events for this study, invite the discussion leader and other members of Group 2 to approve, or use their Bibles and correct, this list. If these members do not detect an error in the sequence which you see exists, lead the class to use their Bibles in correcting this inaccuracy. Later, in discussing small-group assignment 3, you will lead the class to use their Bibles in supplying any *gaps* in this list which members do not point out by that time.

Call now for Group 1 to report on assignment 2. Head a second column on the chalkboard, "Chief Events." With a discussion board, write this heading on a card; the responses "under" this heading simply follow across the board. Or you can use the discussion board in column fashion. Under this heading, however, write the subheadings "Group 1" and "Group 2." The two groups likely will disagree on the five most significant events in the Absalom-David history. Moreover, comparison of the two lists can prove interesting and profitable.

Write key words from Group 1's selection of chief events. Then ask for Group 2's list and write these events in a parallel column. Call attention to any differences in the two lists, but do not encourage depth analysis in this session in view of your information-teaching aim. The next session will be devoted to such analysis and understanding. Moreover, time forbids extension of discussion at this point beyond the knowledge-gaining stage of assignment 2.

Ask the spokesman for Group 1 now to tell what his members discovered in working on assignment 3. Head the third main column on the chalkboard "Questions." Write in abbreviated form those gaps in information or questions of background interpretation raised by Group 1. Then ask Group 2 to add to this list what they feel is needed. With this full list in hand, help both groups to find answers to their questions. Lead members to use their Bibles and other study material at this point. Also, have on hand a copy of the lecturer's background presentation. Use this material, along with your own preparation notes, as you help the class to gain as complete a background of Bible knowledge as is possible in this first session of the unit.

Concluding the Study

The end of the session is near. You now help members to think about the significance of the Bible facts which they have considered. Use *brainstorming* for this purpose. Ask a question like this: What understandings do we need as we continue this unit of study concerning Absalom and David and the child-parent relationship?

Write this heading on the chalkboard or discussion board: "Understandings Needed." Use of a discussion board again enables you easily to preserve the results of this brainstorming for the next session, as does use of newsprint and crayon here instead of the chalkboard. If it is helpful in stimulating responses, call attention to the two columns already written under "Chief Events." Certain understandings are needed in order finally to decide which are the chief events in the Absalom-David relationship.

Call for responses until six or eight suggestions are placed before the class. Then help members to decide which three understandings seem to be the most essential. When these are selected, ask members to reflect upon these relationships before the next class study.

Colloquy

Count on at least an hour for Bible study when you use this teaching approach. For you are securing much class involvement, and on varying levels of study and thought about Christian response. First, members are led to engage in small-group discussion. Then group spokesmen cross mental swords with prepared resource persons. Class members evaluate what is said in this panel discussion. And, finally, you ask members to make personal decisions for action in the area of Bible truth which they are studying. Teaching aim IV is the one which gives guidance to these classroom procedures: *To help class members decide upon ways by which they will seek to deepen the bonds of respect and affection between themselves and their parents.*

Beginning the Study

Perhaps this is the last session in the unit. Relate it closely to the preclass session if it offers helpful motivation for the study. Then use *lecture* to explain the way in which previous studies in the unit have prepared members for this final, implication-filled session. Summarize enough of what members have discovered and agreed upon in previous sessions to offer the needed biblical background for thoughtful reflection and decision making.

Now explain the Bible study procedure which you and the class will follow: small-group study, panel forum, and a period of decision making. Introduce the three or four persons who have agreed to serve as your panel of resource persons. These people may be class members who have made special preparation for this Bible study approach. Or they may be teachers or other qualified persons helping here as team teachers. Then appoint the small groups and ask them to choose group-study leaders. These persons later will act as spokesmen for the groups in the panel discussion, and form Panel 2.

Make assignments to the small groups next. Asking the two groups to take six or eight minutes to phrase some questions concerning Absalom and David for later use often suits your teaching purpose well. But here, expand the assignment. Ask each group to reflect upon five aspects of the biblical situation as it has developed in the studies up to this session. Group members will prepare brief but carefully-thought-out responses to these five questions: (1) What were perhaps the two best opportunities which Absalom and David had for becoming closer and respecting each other more in the months preceding Absalom's death? (2) What was there in his father that Absalom as a young man still could have respected enough to have built a satisfying relationship upon? (3) Why may Absalom have been unable within himself to draw closer to his father? (4) What are two appropriate ways in which one may let his parents know that they are respected by him? (5) What is the main question to answer or obstacle to overcome in successfully assuring parents that they are appreciated and respected?

Now ask the small groups to take about fifteen minutes in order to consider responsibly this rather large assignment. Remember that your resource persons form Panel 1 in the next phase of the colloquy, as we are using the procedure. These people also should use this time to reflect upon the five questions just mentioned, especially questions 3 and 4. They should make notes, check with one another on panel discussion plans, talk with you as moderator on procedure and the Bible insights which already have been recognized by the class, and so on. You also should circulate between the two study groups. Encourage them to move steadily through their questions, and quietly assist in any way that you can.

Going Further in Bible Study

When the two groups have completed work on their assignments, help members to move into the panel forum phase of the colloquy. The two group-study leaders come to the front of the class and sit partially facing Panel 1 and partially facing the rest of the class. They form Panel 2. Panel 1 members, your specially prepared resource persons, sit the same way. Thus panel members can talk back and forth to each other and also see and respond to other class members who react in the forum periods. You, the teacher, serve as moderator and as chief resource person whenever the need arises in the course of the Bible study.

Prepare to use the chalkboard or discussion board to record key words from the small group reports. Now ask the spokesman for Study Group 1 to report what his group decided about question 1. Write his response on the left side of a column numbered "1." Ask the spokesman for Group 2 to give the decision of his group, and write these answers in a column to the right of those named by Group 1. Merely call attention to any differences in these two lists and invite the "audience," the rest of the class, to comment briefly if they wish. Panel 1 is holding its "fire" until the debatable questions—3, 4, and 5—are reported on by members of Panel 2. The achieving of your teaching aim requires that you lead the two panels to concentrate their best thinking—and most time—on these last three questions.

Ask spokesmen for Groups 1 and 2 now to report what they decided about question 2. Again list in parallel columns, under "2" this time, what the groups said. The answers of the two groups concerning question 1 could both differ and complement each other. The responses here just help to produce a longer list of qualities in David which Absalom could have respected, if he had wished to do so. Invite other class members, and Panel 1 also, to add to this list.

Move quickly now to Group 1's report on question 3. Prepare to list these responses under "3" on the chalkboard. Remind the spokesman for Group 1, however, to address his comments to Panel 1, and not to you. Encourage each member of Panel 1 to react to what Group 1's representative says. Invite difference of opinion, use of the Bible and previous studies to support viewpoints, and so on. The other member of Panel 2 supports his partner as far as he conscientiously can do so. Then he brings into the discussion the feelings of Group 2 on the question.

When the two panels seem to have come to the best agreement possible as to whether Absalom was able to bring himself to an attitude of respect for his father, invite other class members to join in the discussion. You, also, should join in now in the solving of this problem. Perhaps you will want to help members see that Absalom probably had not reached the point of no return in controlling his own feelings and actions. A part of your purpose with this question, then, is to help members recognize at this point that they can do what they really want to do. This line of reflection thus prepares the group for the panel discussion of question 4.

Now ask the spokesman for Group 1 to present to Panel 1 his group's answers to question 4. Jot these possible actions down under "4" on the chalkboard. (The discussion board is especially helpful with this question, for retaining the data.) Urge Panel 1 to evaluate the pros and cons of these suggestions carefully. These resource persons should express their opinions as to each suggestion's feasibility, its kindness, its appropriateness, and so on. The two panels even may debate a little on the ideas which Group 1 presented. Then ask the spokesman from Group 2 to offer his proposals for action. Panel 1 subjects these ideas to the same searching (but not negatively critical) examination.

As soon as a thorough sifting of Panel 2's answers to question 4 has occurred, invite the rest of the class to join in the discussion. Call for any additional ways of causing parents actually to know that they are appreciated and respected. Offer your best ideas, also, as another member of the class helping to discover solutions to the problem.

Now request the two group representatives to state to Panel 1 what their groups felt were the main obstacles to overcome in convincing possibly skeptical parents that they are appreciated and respected. Members of Panel 1 then will react sympathetically but quite realistically to these opinions. After the two panels have wrestled with this question for some five minutes, encourage other class members to join in the discussion. Lead the class, then, to come to constructive agreement on what questions one must answer honestly for himself if he is to achieve and maintain the relationship with parents which the class has been discussing.

Concluding the Study

Use *reflection-prayer* now for a full minute. Invite each member silently to pray and to consider what he will do the coming week to cause the parent who needs this more to feel appreciated and respected. Do not put pressure on any individual to reveal his decision.

Merely give each member the opportunity to make this decision inwardly.

Maybe you know your class well, however, and feel that they will respond favorably to a further approach. You now say that genuine spiritual encouragement will come to everyone if one or two members, in the next class session, will share with the class the inner satisfactions which came to them as they followed through upon their decisions. This suggestion does not go so far, perhaps, as to constitute an assignment-report approach on your part. If you and your members have such a relationship that you can challenge them in a friendly manner to a "holy experiment," fine. But your invitation is, rather, an advance invitation to members to bear brief *testimonies* next time concerning what Christ has helped them to do in their response to revealed Bible truth. Nor will this sharing be a checkup, but a rejoicing at what results from reflective, sincere class study of God's Word. Recalling your fourth (action) kind of teaching aim, you will recognize that this final step in leading Bible study reinforces the chances of reaching your spiritual goal during this session. For if members have something thrilling to tell the class next time, you will know that, with the Holy Spirit's help, you achieved some success this time.

Close the session by asking God for divine guidance and support on behalf of class members next week as each person responds in his own way to Christ's will concerning relationship to parents.

5
Leading Discussion

If this book helps you in no other way, it should at least persuade you to introduce discussion into your teaching. Chapter 4 has already touched on some possibilities for using discussion in connection with lecturing. Now, however, we can go a step further. Let us look at discussion as the main teaching plan that you use for an entire session. The present chapter will talk about two ways of going about this—the informal and the formal.

Informal Discussion

Recall the brief description in chapter 2 of the informal discussion as a basic teaching approach. Using this method, you as teacher ask carefully phrased questions which involve the class in Bible examination, analysis, interpretation, and application to their life concerns and relationships. As you and the class discover satisfying answers to these questions, your teaching aim for the session is achieved. The teaching aim which we are using with informal discussion is number IV, application of Bible truth to life relationships. This aim was stated this way in chapter 1: *To help class members decide upon ways by which they will seek to deepen the bonds of respect and affection between themselves and their parents.*

We discussed in chapter 1 the process by which you began a list of potentially profitable questions or spiritual problems for class discussion. As you continued your preparation to teach, you added to this list and possibly revised some questions as you went along. Now you have completed your background preparation and are ready to phrase your questions for actual use in class. Here are some guidelines to help you.

Asking Good Questions

Because your teaching aims will vary, the suggestions which follow apply in varying degrees to your teaching on a given occasion. Some of these guides help more when Bible information is your aim. Others assist best when self-application and conviction are what you seek for class members. Nevertheless, these will serve generally as pointers.

1. Ask questions which indicate to members that you approach class Bible study with an honestly exploring, open mind. Though you have prepared well, you have not come with a prefabricated, predigested "message" or inflexible interpretation of the Scripture passages. While maintaining your role as teacher, you are going to join with class members in discovering, with the Holy Spirit's aid, what Christ is saying to *all* of you through his Word. You may ask: What can be said in favor of Absalom's action, before we form our final conclusion about him? Not: Does anyone here have any doubt that Absalom got what was coming to him?

2. Ask questions which presuppose members' possession of the Bible information which you want them to have. Go one step beyond simply calling for response as to a Bible fact; ask a question which requires members to *use* the fact thoughtfully. Thus, if no one can offer an interpretation of the fact, you and the class have a mature and psychologically motivating reason for going together to the Bible to find it. Ask something like this: What do you think Absalom's feelings and intentions were as he began to place himself before the people on the edge of the city? Not: What did Absalom do in order to get himself before the people?

3. Avoid simple yes-no questions, except on such occasions as taking a survey of members' Bible knowledge or opinions, setting the situation for a thought question immediately to follow, and so on. Don't conduct the class as if you were drilling a class of children on their biblical ABC's!

4. Avoid directing a question of biblical fact or interpretation to a particular class member when you think that, at the moment, he might be unable to answer and thus might be embarrassed. Your purpose is not to pinpoint and publicize the specific biblical ignorance of members. It is to woo them into the experience of spiritually profitable class Bible study.

5. Ask questions which require members to analyze Bible statements, to express approval or disapproval of the clear implications of Bible truth. Use questions which strike a spark of mental challenge and exchange; which invite comparison—even disagreement—with

one another; which require reconciliation of ideas about Bible meanings.

6. Ask a question to start with that goes to the heart of the central truth of the passages. Thus, when you allow plenty of time for exploring possible answers, you aren't "wasting time." You need not feel that you must "get to the lesson." You already have come well along the way toward achieving your teaching aim. You may begin by asking a question like: Why do young persons often feel antagonistic toward their parents? You can see that strong overtones from this lead-off question will remain in members' minds until the end of the session.

7. Ask questions which involve members emotionally. For it is in this way that you draw the heart as well as the head into serious study of God's Word. Ask youth or young adults: What possibly were some of Absalom's feelings as he plotted and rebelled against his father? Not: What were the things that Absalom did in plotting against his father?

8. Avoid preachy questions. Questions should honestly seek information, call for interpretation, or give opportunity for genuine response as to members' opinions or feelings. They should not be used to moralize, which can be done honestly and directly if done at all. Ask young persons: In what ways, in his rebellion, may Absalom have hurt David? Not: Should Absalom have treated David like he did, no matter what David's sins were?

9. Avoid "whipping" questions. If class members do not like to be preached at in the guise of questions, neither do they want to be chastened with questions. Ask members: What can it do to a young person who comes to feel like Absalom felt and who becomes involved in undermining and fighting his father? Not: What kind of sinful impulses cause a young person to undermine his father as Absalom did?

10. Ask questions which lead members to think in constructive terms rather than in negative terms. Ask class members: How can one actually cause a parent to feel respected? Not: Why will some of us never get around to making an effort at showing respect for our fathers and mothers?

11. Ask questions about what members can do *now,* not about what they should have done in some past failures. Thinking of now and the future in obeying Christ is more spiritually profitable than dwelling on the depressing past.

12. At each stage of the Bible study session ask the question which will accomplish what you desire.[1] Certain questions will *open up* class discussion, such as: First, then, what may have been some of the main problems which existed between Absalom and his father? Other questions will *broaden class participation,* like: Before we go further, what do all of us think about David's decision to retreat from Jerusalem? To *limit participation,* ask a question like: Before we go on, Joe, will you relate to us exactly how *you* felt when your parent once did something like this? You can *focus discussion* with a question like: Taking into consideration all that we have said, what do you say was Absalom's main, deep, underlying attitude toward David? And you can *aid continuity* between class sessions with questions like: In view of what we agreed upon last time about David as the father of the *boy* Absalom, what can we expect Absalom to feel toward David as we find them in this passage?

Beginning the Study

Now you are ready to imagine yourself assuming leadership of the class. At times we shall use a *thinking-out-loud* approach to the use of various questions and teaching procedures.

As you begin, use *lecture* to tie in mentally and emotionally with what has been said in the preclass period with reference to this Bible study. As you do this, refer to some current item of news or a recent significant event in the church or community. Even the tragic fact of some young man who has rebelled violently against one or both parents will serve at this point to show the relevance of this Bible study. State that the news item shows how prominent in young adults' lives today are the human problems dealt with in the Bible passages before you in this study.

Remind members next of this biblical or unit sequence which you are following. Summarize in about one minute the substance of class discussion during the last session, doing this in terms which show how the Bible study to follow will help to solve some unanswered problems from last time.

Strike right through the central truth of these passages in 2 Samuel (15:1–12 and 18:31–33) with a question which at the same time

---

[1] See, also, A. R. and H. B. Trecker, *How to Work with Groups* (New York: Association Press, 1958), pp. 69–71.

shows how close to class members' lives this study will come. Ask a question like: *What would you like most to have that belongs to your father?* You can see that here is a question almost any member can answer, no matter how little Bible knowledge he has. And this question leads directly to a close look at Absalom. Moreover, this question just might get near a sensitive spot with some class members where the assistance of this Bible study is needed.

Also, this question is rather personal. In order to get the most involvement here at the start, use an *unsigned written survey* by which members may respond to your question. Hand out slips of paper and pencils to all members. Ask the class to reflect quietly for some thirty to sixty seconds. Perhaps they will want to close their eyes and visualize the home situation as best they can imagine it. Encourage every person to write down something—the best answer he can make to the question. After all members who are going to participate at this point have finished, collect the responses.

Scan each response to pull out the key word or phrase, then quickly write all responses in a column on one side of the chalkboard or discussion board. Words such as "his car," "his money," "his reputation," "his job," may turn up. Check or underscore the ones of these anonymous but expressed desires for father's possessions which relate most to Absalom's desires (David's throne, his wives, his reputation, and so on). Do not draw these comparisons at this point, however. Simply say that these underscored objects of desire may be quite natural and suggest that similar desires may have troubled Absalom. State that all of you now will proceed to explore Absalom's dilemma and that you will return to the chalkboard list later.

Next, ask a question like this: *What do you think Absalom's feelings and intentions were as he began to place himself before the people on the edge of the city?* With this question, you begin to turn members' attention to essential details of the Bible passage. If some in the class have made advance preparation, lead discussion toward answering this second question. Write key words in all responses on the chalkboard in recognition of thoughtful participation and for use later in the session. Call attention to any responses here which relate to the list already on the chalkboard.

If members are vague as to what you are referring to, here is your chance immediately to use *classroom Bible research* as you direct attention to the Scriptures and to certain facts about Absalom's actions. But even if a few members are prepared to discuss this question in a rather informed way, you will come to a point soon where more biblical background and interpretation is needed if the whole class is to become involved with Absalom and his relationship to David.

Going Further in Bible Study

At this stage you well may need to ask a question like: *What Bible background do we need in order to give Absalom his due?* At this point in class discussion you are helping members to focus mentally and emotionally upon some key Bible truths which will be needed later in the session. Your young adults need to identify with Absalom in order to decide best, later, how he went the wrong way. You may use *lecture, leading questions,* and *Bible research* to bring out David's polygamy, his great sin with Bathsheba, Absalom's heathen ancestry, Absalom's murder of his half-brother Amnon, his self-exile to escape death and banishment from the palace for two years after being allowed to return to Jerusalem, his fear of not being appointed heir to David even though now the oldest son and of royal ancestry on both sides, and so on.

After this highly selective Bible study, help members to begin thinking both about what happened within Absalom and about what may be happening within themselves with relation to their own parents. Ask a question like: *What can it do to a young person who comes to feel like Absalom felt and who becomes involved in undermining and fighting his father?* Guide responses so that members will comment in terms of young adults *today,* not just as an analysis of what Absalom reflected. Here you help the class to think through the bonds of love which may lie deep, even though dormant, within a young man and his father because of childhood experiences. What does it do to a young person to try cutting these bonds violently and dishonorably? And even if not many happy childhood experiences occurred, what still are these bonds between young person and parent? Help the class to explore what Absalom did to himself, and what anyone does to himself who rejects and seeks to "kill" his parents.

You may recognize how extended this phase of class study can become. You thought this time factor through, of course, as you made your teaching plan. You may want to take more time here and less time on other questions. Another teacher may make a different time allocation for this penetrating question. But a question like this prepares for the last phase of this Bible study session.

Concluding the Study

You now have some fifteen minutes remaining in which to help class members think seriously about how they will face up to the Bible truth they have discovered and analyzed. How do they apply this truth to themselves? What do they intend to do? How will they begin? (Remember your teaching aim.)

Help members begin to think and feel along these lines by asking a question like this: *Where were some of the perhaps good chances for David and Absalom, in the months preceding Absalom's death, to become closer and more respecting of each other?* You may have to repeat some of the events in Absalom's life, or draw out these events from members if they can offer them readily. Use these experiences for exploring answers to this question. One of the times which you and the class may discuss was the two-year period when Absalom had returned from self-exile, was living right in Jerusalem, but he and his father never saw each other. Use *brainstorming* to help the class discuss what Absalom and David might have done during these two years, why they didn't do it, and so on. Make two columns on the chalkboard, heading them "David" and "Absalom." List under each heading what each possibly could have done toward achieving reconciliation.

After about five minutes, ask: *What can a son (or daughter) do to develop in his heart more feeling of respect for his parents?* Again use *brainstorming* and the chalkboard to explore possible answers to this problem. This question calls for even more reflection upon one's own home situation. Class members' own attitudes toward their parents are involved here. How these attitudes can be changed by members themselves, wherever change is needed, is the question. Again write responses on the chalkboard in abbreviated form for later use, as before, whenever the succeeding class discussion makes reference to these responses appropriate. (Whenever you base a comment of your own upon these chalkboard notes, you strengthen the validity of your statement in members' minds.)

Another question which likely should be asked is: *In what ways can one actually cause parents to know they are respected?* The brainstorming, analysis, and summarizing of responses at this stage need not be extended. Soon you are going to ask the question which puts the matter squarely up to each class member and leaves it there with him and his Christ.

Now ask a question like this: *In what way will you do something this week to cause a possibly neglected parent to know he (or she) is respected?* Of course, you are not going to try to force, in any manner, a verbal response from anyone. Outward responses have been plentiful, and possibilities have been explored. Now use *reflection-prayer* to help members face themselves and their parents in the presence of Christ. Ask the class if each one silently will think about the parent who most needs his respect. Ask members each to pray for his parent in this special need. Then ask each one prayerfully to decide in his own mind and heart what he is going to do during the coming week to let this parent know that he respects and appreciates him for certain things.

After one or two minutes of silent reflection and prayer, lead the class in a brief prayer closing the session of Bible study.

This treatment of informal discussion has been longer than that which will be used with some other teaching methods. This is our first plunge in this fashion into the Bible material and into the life concerns and response possibilities of your class members. Eight thought-provoking questions have been used. You can deal effectively in forty-five minutes with eight questions like these. Or you can use these eight in combinations in thirty minutes or less. As you see, no matter what Bible-content type of question you omit in order to use fewer questions, you still need to help members gain certain basic Bible knowledge. Under certain circumstances, where interest in the study already is established, the first question using unsigned responses can be omitted, saving some five minutes. Another series of questions will take you in another direction toward achieving the same teaching aim. Maybe a series containing fewer questions suits you better. For instance, you can use questions 3, 4, 5, 6, 7, and 8 and travel over substantially the same course of Bible study. The time factor always will tell you how few and thus how inclusive those questions should be which involve Bible content.

Formal Discussion

Recall from chapter 1 that formal discussion is group problem solving carried out in a logical manner. In our Bible study situation, the problem for study corresponds to your teaching aim. When you use this discussion type of teaching procedure, then: (1) you state the problem for study; (2) you help members to single out pertinent Bible facts and life situation factors; (3) you help the class to determine possible solutions to the Bible study problem; (4) you lead members to consider the advantages and disadvantages of each solution; and (5) you help members to select a solution of their own in light of all the considerations.

You can see that this teaching approach is purposeful. It also can foster maturity in Bible study on the part of your class, for the classroom process is "low temperature." If class temperature is high, if members already are emotionally aroused over some of the issues unavoidably involved in studying a given passage of Scripture, this approach to Bible study can slow down thoughts and emotions, lower the class temperature, and foster thoughtful study of provocative spiritual truths.

Beginning the Study

As you begin this session, use *lecture* to tie in with any preclass emphasis which has been made. Relate this Bible study to those which have preceded. Then tell the class that you are proposing a very thoroughgoing approach to Bible study for this session. State that the ultimate problem or question in this topic, as the unit has been developed, is: *What is the best way this week that I can deepen the bonds of respect and affection between myself and my parents?* (You recognize this as teaching aim IV.) Then explain the steps you and the class will follow in your Bible research, analysis, and decision making.

Now you move into step 2 of this adaptation of formal discussion. Use *brainstorming* as you ask members to suggest the various areas of Bible knowledge and son-father relationships which should be discussed briefly in order to move intelligently into the study. Lead members to think creatively along the lines of Absalom's parentage and childhood; his brother-sister-parent relationships; his ambitions and frustrations; his possible shame over his father David's behavior (see 2 Samuel 15); his murder of Amnon and self-exile; his craftiness; his possible virtues; David's decline in several respects; his continuing love for Absalom; the virtues in David which Absalom still could have respected; Absalom's possible inability now to show respect for his father; and class-member-centered factors such as whether a son must undermine his father in order to achieve his goals, whether a parent's neglect and failure with a son means that he does not love his child, and so on.

Record in a column on the chalkboard or discussion board key words from these basic ideas which you and the class produce as a result of your advance study, present Bible searching, and reflection. Lead the class briefly to pinpoint possibly the best chance, in the series of events just discussed, for Absalom and David to have drawn closer together. One of these times may have been the two years while Absalom was in Jerusalem after being allowed to return from flight in Syria.

Going Further in Bible Study

Now use *circular response* in step 3 of your teaching approach. Start with a member who likely will respond readily and thoughtfully. Ask him, and each one around the circle, to suggest one way in which a young person in their situation can cause parents to know they are respected. Accept each idea fully, allow no reaction to suggestions, and write responses in a column on the chalkboard.

Next mark off the class in half. Ask Side 1 to reflect briefly upon one advantage of each suggested solution just written on the chalkboard. Ask Side 2 to think of one disadvantage of each suggestion just listed. If you have enough members on each side, you might shorten the reflection time required by assigning one suggestion to each person. After some two or three minutes of reflection, call for members to evaluate the proposed solutions as to advantages and disadvantages. Because of the probable time factor, simply receive each evaluation without further discussion. Each member will make his own decision anyway.

Concluding the Study

Now use a *written, unsigned survey of the class* to give opportunity to each member to make his decision between himself and his Christ. Hand out pencils and slips of paper to each member. Appeal to each member to write his best answer to the original Bible-study problem with which you began the session. Read it again slowly and clearly. Allow a minute or two for reflection and writing. You can ask members to fold their papers and hand them in to you as objects of your specific and personal prayer this week. Or you can ask members to keep their written decisions as reminders of what they have said they will do this week.

Close with a minute of *reflection* by each member upon how he will go about carrying out his decision. Then lead in prayer for the Holy Spirit's prompting, guidance, and blessing.

6
Informal Forums

As we saw in chapter 4, a forum is one important way to introduce variety and secure discussion in connection with lecture teaching. It is quite possible, however, to use some type of forum as the main approach around which an entire teaching session is built. This chapter and the next one will describe several kinds of forums that can be used in this way. The types to be discussed in the present chapter are called "informal" for a simple reason. Only you, the teacher or study leader, must make specific preparation for them in advance. You, of course, must plan and prepare carefully, but you may not enlist additional help beforehand. By contrast, the so-called "feature" forums to be described in chapter 7 often involve getting others to prepare in advance or help arrange some kind of program feature such as a visual aid.

Classroom Bible Research Forum

This first of the informal forums to be considered involves "pure" Bible study. As you have seen in chapter 2, you lead the class to explore what God's Word says, what it means, and what significance it has for you and your members today. To aid your study, bring to class Bible commentaries, Bible dictionaries, and other such study aids. Then lead the class to engage in a type of workshop in Bible study.

You still use a teaching aim, of course. And you still are at a certain point in your unit of Bible study. Perhaps a good aim to use in order to see the possibilities of this teaching procedure is aim II: *To help class members understand and appreciate the significance of the experiences which Absalom and David had as son and father.* Turn back to chapter 1 if you wish to review the role which this kind of teaching aim plays in a total unit of Bible study. You are not avoiding the development of conviction and the achieving of response to Bible truth, but you are not seeking it specifically in this session.

Beginning the Study

Begin class Bible study by tying in with the preclass period as you do with lecture forum. The same type of "high temperature" beginning aids you with this teaching procedure as it does with lecture forum. Class members need strong motivation in this day to embark enthusiastically upon a session of intense Bible searching and analysis. They need to feel the critical timeliness, the high value, of such an endeavor. You no doubt do have some class members who have this conviction about the value of thoughtful Bible study.

A unit chart seems quite appropriate for this academic approach to Bible study. You may use this chart and *lecture,* in fact, to review the biblical setting briefly and to show that this session of Bible exploration and analysis will lead later in the unit to studies about personal convictions and personal actions.

Ask the class what areas of biblical background they feel they need in order to understand Absalom, David, and their relationship as son and father. Use a type of *brainstorming* to get at this problem, listing in a column on the chalkboard or discussion board key words from each response. No doubt factors will be suggested like Absalom's parentage, his childhood experiences with David, his personal appearance, his relationships with brothers and sisters, his personal ambitions and good intentions, his mistakes, his virtues, David's mistakes with Absalom and with others, his virtues; and so on. You may have to help members, at first, to think in the terms you are calling for. Leave these points of Bible information on the chalkboard, for you and the class are about to place beside each factor in the biblical situation the Scripture references offering help at that point.

Perhaps the elements listed on the chalkboard which the class has said affected Absalom's relationship with his father David are not listed in chronological order. If you wish to study these influencing factors in a loosely arranged chronological order, help the class to decide upon this order. Or, you and the class may wish to take up the points in some other order. Number the situations or events in the order that members feel offers the most satisfying sequence for study. Discourage technical, dogmatic argument over which factor should come where in the list. For who could say for sure about this?

Going Further in Bible Study

Now help members to prepare their Bibles, Bible dictionaries, and other resource books for careful study. Ask everyone to open Bibles to 2 Samuel as a starting place. Call attention to factor number 1 on your chalkboard list and ask members to locate the Scripture passages which offer information on the point. In this process, you may assign different factors to different class members for researching. If you choose to ask all members to determine the Bible data for each point, be sure to rotate the privilege of reporting what has been discovered. Moreover, you may be using a *workbook* approach in this session whereby each member writes down what he discovers. You later can rotate more easily the privilege of reporting findings to the class if members have recorded the information they have discovered. Suggest that they look in their Bible dictionaries and other indexed resource books for topics like "Absalom," "David," "Amnon," and so on.

Whenever you do call for reports on the passages being sought, write these references on the chalkboard in a second column and beside the proper factor in the first column. And when you go on to help the class decide what the passages say in explanation of the points in column 1, write this information briefly on the same line in a third column.

Thus you and the class use the chalkboard to develop your results in Bible research something like this:

1. Absalom's parentage—2 Samuel 3:3—mother, heathen, daughter of a king, . . .
2. Absalom's homelife—2 Samuel 3:2–5—half-brothers, jealousy, rivalry, heathenism, . . .
3. Absalom's frustrations—2 Samuel 14:24—allowed in Jerusalem but not allowed to see his father, . . .

You see that this example omits several significant events between factors two and three. Your own prior Bible study will have prepared you to guide in completing this chart of Bible information. The Bible dictionaries and other resource books are sufficiently helpful so that this process may not require over fifteen minutes if you and the class develop only those factors which bear most clearly upon your research purpose.

With this Bible analysis as a background, lead members through *reflection-response* to consider a Bible study problem like this: *In view of what we can see from Absalom's earlier life, what can we expect him to feel toward his father as we find them in 2 Samuel 15?* Class members' responses here may amount in some measure to a summary of data on the chalkboard. In spite of what has or has not been said so far, however, establish clearly Absalom's possible resentment, his scorn of an aged and compromised father, his anxiety and mistrust of David's intentions toward him, his arrogance regarding his father-king, his utter lack of ethical principles regarding his father, and so on.

Now you are ready to ask a key question for your young adults to ponder: What could Absalom have blamed his father for, as later he was dying, and what must he have blamed himself for? You see what bearing thoughtful discussion of this question has on your teaching aim. A major concern for your members is not "blame," of course, but the responsibility which a young person must take for himself even after he realizes in what sense his parent has failed him. Moreover, your purpose here is not to lead the class to arrive at a conclusive answer as to exact degrees of blame, for this cannot be done. You seek, rather, to help members think deeply about how closely their lives have been intertwined with the personalities of their parents and yet about their own responsibility for themselves before God.

In order to stimulate hard thinking, divide the class in half. Ask Group 1 to review silently the Bible data compiled on the chalkboard during the session and to reflect individually upon those aspects of Absalom's calamity which seem to have come from David's wrongdoing and neglect through the years. Ask Group 2 to reflect upon those aspects of Absalom's bitter life and fate which seem to have resulted from Absalom's own weakness and wrongdoing. Members may want to jot down their thoughts for accurate recall in a few moments. After some two minutes of silent reflection, ask all members in Group 1 to give the results of their thinking as you write in one column on the chalkboard key words or phrases from each response. Then ask class members in Group 2 to express what they decided about Absalom's responsibility. Record key parts of these responses in a second column on the chalkboard.

Lead the class as a whole to compare the judgments of the two halves of the class. Do any differences of feeling exist? Maintaining a friendly atmosphere throughout, seek general agreement at specific points as to whether Absalom alone was to blame or whether David also contributed significantly.

The processes in Bible research and analysis which we have dealt with here may require all the time you have in class session. And even if you have more time available, there is something to be said for leaving your class members in a kind of learning suspense, as you use this number II teaching aim. You still have one or more sessions in which to foster conviction and first steps in outward response to Bible truth.

Concluding the Study

Suppose you have some time available. You may feel that you wish to close this session on what seems to you a more positive note. Here is a good way to follow up on the Bible study which the class has done to this point. Ask a final question like this: Based on the Bible research and analysis which we have done, what do you say there was remaining in his father David at the time of Absalom's rebellion that Absalom still could have respected deeply if he had wanted to do so? Find a place on the crowded chalkboard—or use some auxiliary newsprint or a discussion board—to list these redeeming features in David's character and situation as members reflect and then name them. Lead the class in a closing prayer asking for Christ's insight and patience as class members set out to understand and to appreciate the role of their parents in a more thoughtful way than ever before.

Case-Study Forum

You may use this informal forum when you want to deepen members' understanding of Bible truth and help them to see the relevance of God's Word for their lives. The true-to-life case of someone you know or have read about involves members mentally and emotionally with issues similar to the ones dealt with in the Bible passages. The class Bible study process thus involves seeking solutions to the life situations in the case you present, in the Bible passages, and in similar situations which exist in your class members' own experiences. Teaching aim II helps explore some of the possibilities of this teaching approach: *To help class members understand and appreciate the significance of the experiences which Absalom and David had as son and father.*

Beginning the Study

Assume that you are teaching a new class or starting a new course of Bible study. Or assume that you feel cautious about getting deeply into this potentially sensitive subject of son/daughter-parent relationships. You want to start slowly. You want to help the class warm up to the deeper levels of this subject. You wish to help members develop an ease in talking frankly about this very personal relationship. Use *group conversation* to develop a relaxed atmosphere for talking to one another.

Start the conversation off as casually as you can by addressing one who responds readily. Ask him if he remembers, as a small boy, who it was in the neighborhood that he looked up to with the most awe. Perhaps it was an older boy who could scale fences, swing from trees, carry the smaller boys on his bicycle, and so on. Allow the conversation along this line to become as spontaneous and undirected as possible. If comments lag or if conversation strays away from the subject, join in quietly and help to continue this reminiscing about childhood and looking up to older, stronger persons in the neighborhood.

You are doing at least two things here: You are encouraging members to talk informally and freely about experiences in childhood. Soon they will be talking about a relationship that goes back to childhood. And you are helping members to begin thinking in terms of looking up to someone, of respecting him. This attitude will become a key issue in the Bible study soon to follow.

Perhaps your members now have felt the experience of going back in memory to childhood and of talking with one another about it. Now tie in naturally to the preclass session emphasis, if this is helpful to your teaching purpose. Also relate the group comments in some natural way to your unit of Bible study and to the topic which you and the class are about to focus upon. Say something like: Well, actually, what we are studying here today with Absalom and David contains clear overtones of what happened in Absalom's own childhood.

Then state that before going further into the session, you want to appoint two *reaction groups* by marking off the class in half. Ask

Group 1 to listen closely to the brief case or life situation which you are about to present. These members later will pinpoint everything they can in Joe's favor, and will say where the father was at fault. Group 2 will listen with the purpose of identifying everything possible in defense of the father, and will say where Joe was at fault. Then place the life situation before the class.

You may have distributed the case to members at the close of the last session and appointed the two reaction groups as just described. If you did this, you are ready to lead members in an analysis of the situation.

But suppose you have planned to present the case to members in this session. Hand out duplicated copies of the brief case description. Allow two or three minutes for members to read the facts. Or, present the situation verbally to the class by reading it, playing it from a pre-recorded disc or tape, or telling it well as a result of careful preparation. Use a case like this:

Ever since Joe could remember, his father had been involved in some big project. When he was at home, he always acted interested in Joe. But there never was time for this interest to develop into anything that Joe could remember. Most of the family decisions of a day-by-day nature were made by Joe's mother. When family discussions took place, Joe's father usually had to give up his viewpoint on the ground that he seldom was home, didn't understand how things were, and was not the parent who would have to make the decision work.

Now Joe, his father, and the whole family had come to a crisis point. Joe was in his second year at college, but home now for Thanksgiving holidays. His father was about to lose his job because he was "cracking up." Aside from what all this meant personally to everyone, Joe was faced with having to drop out of college and the whole family was faced with loss of their home.

The trouble with Joe's father, it seemed, was that he had lost all confidence in himself. He was nothing of the salesman he once had been. He felt that no one appreciated him or trusted what he had to say. As a counselor soon discovered, Joe's father felt that his own family did not respect him, especially Joe and Joe's younger brother and sister. The father's desire to succeed and his will to keep trying was gone. The drinking to which he had turned added to the problem for the whole family. Now Joe's mother was trying to discover where the answer was for her husband and for all of them. Their pastor was anxious to be as helpful as possible to a family, all of whose members had been regular attenders in church for years.

If you present the case verbally, pause after you have finished to make sure that everyone understands the facts as given. In later discussion, hold comments as reasonably as possible to these facts. Now lead all members to join in pointing out some factors in the family situation which seem to have important bearings on the problem of the father, Joe, Joe's brother and sister, and their total relationship with each other through the years. Caution your two reaction groups to withhold their defense and evaluation of the father and Joe until the class has noted these general factors in the family situation. Write these general observations on the chalkboard for later relating to what the reaction groups say. The type of comments which members might make here are: "The mother had to make too many decisions." "They all went to church regularly." "The pastor wanted to help." "The father's business was slacking off." Notice that you are not leading members to offer final judgments, but simply to recognize all factors in the case. The class will use these factors, placed before them on the chalkboard, in evaluating the tentative conclusions of the two reaction groups.

Now ask various members of Group 1 to sum up all aspects of the family situation which seem to excuse Joe from fault in the present tragic condition of his father. They will of necessity comment on the factors which seem to say that the father is almost wholly responsible for his present condition. Do not allow general evaluation of Group 1's conclusions. Let matters regarding this side of the case remain unsolved. Good final conclusions cannot be arrived at until helpful Bible passages have been examined and interpreted.

Now call for persons in Group 2 to say what they can in defense of the father. They will point out everything which seems to say that Joe could have gone far toward helping his father develop his feeling of self-respect, of being appreciated, and of optimism regarding his work. Postpone any effort to take issue with Group 2's conclusions.

Now bring Bible information to bear upon the case. Use *lecture* to show a situation existing between Absalom and David which had elements in it similar to those in the case just examined. Give to the class a brief historical account of Absalom's parentage, early home-life, brothers and sisters, probable lack of association with his father

David, jealousy in the family, murder of Amnon, flight, return but isolation from his father, plotting, rebellion, craftiness, and death. Include other details which should help your class members to feel something of the relationship which existed between Absalom and David. Points in David's behalf certainly are necessary, such as the signs of David's affection for Absalom and the genuine problems which David had as king.

Going Further in Bible Study

Now ask Groups 1 and 2 to form in small circles and quickly choose a discussion leader. Each group is going to seek answers briefly to two questions arising out of the Bible data you have described. Then they will agree on some tentative conclusions. Ask Group 1 to agree upon answers to these two questions: (1) What feelings may have prompted Absalom to set out upon the course of rebellion that he chose? (2) What can be said in favor of Absalom's actions in rebelling against his father? Group 1 also will go further and seek to agree on a third point: the various ways in which David was at fault in Absalom's tragic fate.

Ask Group 2 to seek agreement on these two questions: (1) What can it do to a young person who comes to feel like Absalom felt and who starts undermining and fighting his father? (2) What was there in his father David that Absalom as a young man still could have respected enough to have built a satisfying relationship upon? Group 2 also will go further and seek agreement on a third point: the various ways in which Absalom alone was to blame for his tragic fate. Allow the two groups about ten minutes to arrive at their answers to the three problems they are to reflect upon.

Your teaching situation may make this small group study a serious time factor. If this is true, simply ask members of the two groups to reflect briefly as they sit in the large group and respond to their questions as you state them one by one. Call for brief group reaction after each question so that members' thinking on one question will contribute to the answering of the next question.

After the two small groups have finished their deliberation, have them regroup in the larger circle. Then call for the discussion leader of Group 1 to report the thinking and feeling of his members. Record in a column on the chalkboard key words and phrases from the group's answers to the three points, simply numbering the three clusters of responses 1-2-3 to save time. Without general reaction at this point, ask Group 2 to report. Write their responses on the chalkboard in a second column so that opinions can be compared easily. Then lead the class to compare the two groups of responses, question by question, wherever parallel points are involved.

Soon you and the class will come to a point in this general discussion when the class begins to acknowledge the responsibility which Absalom must have accepted for his tragic fate, if he had been disposed to do so. Now ask a preenlisted class member if he will tell the class something which he has told you during the past week. Thus you use a *testimony* through which one of your young adults helps the whole class to appreciate what respecting, loving relationships with a father means. This testimony should be true, of course. You would have to know your class members well enough that you could select one who genuinely could share with others what the close relationship with his father has meant to him *in recent months of trial.* (Remember your teaching aim.) This testimony will help to clarify what Absalom needed so desperately and did not find.

Concluding the Study

Now use *brainstorming* briefly to help the class solve two final problems in child-parent relationships. As they think of Absalom and David, they will inevitably gain understanding of their own family relationships. First ask members: What were some of the perhaps good chances for David and Absalom, in the months preceding Absalom's death, to become closer and more respecting of each other? List these occasions on the chalkboard as members reflect briefly and suggest them.

Then ask the class to think of Joe and his father, and of young persons today. Request members to suggest, in light of what Groups 1 and 2 have said, what Joe could have done in order to have cultivated in himself a deeper awareness of and appreciation of what his father could mean to him. (Remember that you are teaching toward a number II aim in this session. Ask members about deep respect, conviction, and action in later sessions, using aims III and IV.) Write on the chalkboard what members offer in Joe's case.

Finally, ask the class what opportunities they have today to develop their own appreciation of what the child-parent relationship means in their lives. Reflection, study, prayer, perhaps talking with parents about early childhood experiences, and similar opportunities may be mentioned. These responses may lodge in members' hearts and perhaps need not be listed on the chalkboard. Close with prayer for the Holy Spirit's inspiration as deeper insights and appreciations for parents are sought by everyone in the class.

Small-Group Study Forum

We have used small-group study already as a supplementary teaching procedure. But here you may allow class members to experience more fully the unique learning experiences which small-group study provides. More time in this session will be devoted to this phase of the Bible study than to any other phase. And time is what is required for the small-group approach to succeed. Class members find it hard to "hurry up and think." We are using teaching aim II here, for this teaching procedure is excellent for *helping members to gain understanding and appreciation of the child-parent relationship.*

Beginning the Study

Use *group conversation* to help class members warm up to talking easily and honestly with each other. Recall how you employed this supplementary procedure in beginning the session when you used the case study forum. Since you want members to communicate willingly and accurately in small groups, lead them to begin doing this as the session is starting.

If the preclass session was planned to highlight some issue or problem which could arise later in Bible study, use *lecture* to relate in some natural way what was said then to what is being said now in class. If preparation for the Bible study session was not accomplished in the earlier period, use a newspaper clipping or other means of showing the relevance of the topic for study. Then point out on a chart or tell how this class session relates to previous Bible studies in the unit.

To further stimulate mental and emotional involvement with this "low temperature" teaching aim, employ *role playing.* Explain the role-play situation carefully. A young adult about twenty years of age has finished high school and is working in his father's store. Increasingly he resents being dominated by his father in the store and at home, where he still lives with his parents. He clashes with his father over store practices. He resents being denied a loan from his father so he can buy his own car, and so on. The father wants to be a good parent but doesn't understand his son's feelings. Thus they often exchange unkind words.

Allow the two members whom you have selected as role players to go outside the room for two or three minutes so they can get together on about four distinct points of difference. Player 1, the son, will prepare to maintain his resentful, rebellious attitude throughout the heated exchange. Player 2 will reflect briefly on how to hold strictly to the role which you have assigned him as the father. While the two members are outside agreeing generally on their points of difference and how to begin, brief the rest of the class on how to evaluate the role playing. Ask them to pay special attention to the interpretation which Player 1 makes of the son. Later, they will discuss thoroughly how true the role playing was to the temperament agreed upon for the son. And they will need to recall other aspects of the son's nature as portrayed by Player 1.

Now call back the two role players and invite them to begin. Much can be said in a short time. So after about three minutes, when you feel that the attitudes of the son and the father have been interpreted as well as the two members are going to do, interrupt the role playing. Express appreciation to the two members for helping thus to open up this son-father conflict for the class. Then divide the class in half, or otherwise form two or more small groups of not more than six members each. Assume here that you have two small groups.

Going Further in Bible Study

Ask each group to choose a study leader who will keep notes and later will report to the whole class. Then assign two tasks to Group 1 at this time. They will evaluate quickly the role playing, determining to what extent full resentment and rebellion were portrayed by Player 1 and agreeing upon how accurate was the portrayal of the father by Player 2. Only about five minutes should be used for this evaluation.

Next, Group 1 will examine quickly the biblical data on Absalom. Supply group members with Scripture references which they may overlook, as you note quietly from time to time how they are progressing. Bible dictionaries also will assist at this stage of group study.

And now this is the last part of Group 1's second assignment: To agree upon the ways in which Absalom was different from the role-play son in attitude toward his father.

After Group 1 members have spent some fifteen minutes completing their two assignments, use *picture study* to help them understand better the emotional and mental state to which Absalom had come by the time of his rebellion. Show to Group 1 three portraits or photographs of young men with pronounced features. Portrayals may show one serene, another mildly troubled, another deeply agitated, another intensely determined, or persons with two or three degrees of troubled personality. Great paintings of Alexander the Great, Judas, the disciple John, and so on, serve your purpose well. Leave the pictures with Group 1 and ask them to agree on which portrayal comes closest to being "Absalom."

After giving Group 1 their assignment, ask Group 2 to evaluate the role playing in the same way that Group 1 evaluated it. Then ask Group 2 to study briefly the biographical data on David and Absalom. They will locate in the Bible the various occasions when the lives of father and son came together. Then they will suggest why the contacts of father and son on each occasion did not yield better results in terms of mutual respect and affection.

Concluding the Study

After some twenty minutes of small group study, regroup the class in a circle. Call for the study leader from Group 1 to tell briefly what his group decided about the faithfulness of the role playing. Next, ask him to explain the ways in which his members feel that Absalom was different from the son in the role playing. Then ask him to show all three pictures to Group 2 and to say which one his group felt most closely pictured Absalom, and why.

Turn then and call for Group 2's responses to their two assignments. If time permits, invite Group 2 now to react briefly to Group 1's findings, and vice versa. By the time this process is over, your class members are sure to have gained insights into what the relationship of son and father might have meant to Absalom and David. Close with a minute of silent reflection upon what it means for one to be the child of his parent. Then pray for the Holy Spirit's guidance and inspiration in this matter of appreciating child-parent ties.

Drama Forum

Among informal forums, *role playing* is a type of drama which helps you significantly with this Bible theme. For role playing is unique in aiding a class to explore the deep involvements of human conflict and love such as existed between Absalom and David. *Impromptu Scripture interpretation* through drama also contributes much to the study of this topic.

Further, these forms of drama help lead class Bible study, under teaching aim III, to go beyond understanding to inner change and conviction forming. This aim may read as follows: *To help class members, in light of the experiences of Absalom and David, to strengthen their convictions about respecting and loving their parents.*

Beginning the Study

Begin the session by relating to the preclass period and to the studies which have preceded in the unit. This is a rather "high temperature" teaching procedure. Therefore, you may use a beginning similar to the one used with informal discussion, minus any reference to local events involving child-parent conflict. Your role playing soon will perform the task of helping the class become involved mentally and emotionally in the Bible study.

Now use role playing as you used it with the small-group study forum. The same son-father conflict situation serves well here. But do not use small groups to evaluate the role playing. Lead members first to react to the degree of resentment and rebellion portrayed by the son. Encourage any suggestions as to how a truer emotional rebellion could have been portrayed by the role player. Did Player 1 slip out of his role at any time? In what ways did the son resent and rebel against his father?

Then help the class to analyze the portrayal of the father. Was his well-meaning but misguided attitude faithfully interpreted? How could he have been portrayed more accurately? In what ways did the father utterly misunderstand his son? After leading the class to evaluate the role playing along these lines, move away from this situation for a time.

Lecture briefly, now. Since you and the class have quickly struck an issue on son-father relationships, you are ready to explore the insights which God's Word can offer. State that events in the lives of Absalom and his father David reflect some parallels with the situation you have just discussed. Continue lecturing by relating in quick sequence the biblical facts connecting Absalom and his father. These range, of course, all the way from Absalom's ancestry to his death and David's lament. Include every sign of David's affection for his son, such as his consent for Absalom to return after he had murdered Amnon and had fled to his mother's people.

Going Further in Bible Study

Lead the class now to focus their best thought on the Bible facts you have just presented. Ask members to analyze how the son, as role-played earlier in the session, differs from Absalom as the Scriptures present him. Write on the chalkboard the key word or phrase from each member's response. These points of difference might be listed in a column under the heading "Sons Differ." Help members to identify such differences as the role-play son's Christian mother versus Absalom's heathen mother, the role-play son's attitude and actions versus those of Absalom, and so on.

Then lead members to suggest differences between David as presented in the Scriptures at this time and the role-play father as portrayed in the class. List responses under the heading, "Fathers Differ." Members may point out such factors as David's probable neglect of Absalom as Absalom was growing up (partly because of the religiously diverse household and David's kingly duties) versus the role-play son's likely closer companionship with his father; David's apparent lack of contact with Absalom as a young man versus the role-play father's close supervision, and so on. In this comparison process, be sure the class identifies as clearly as possible Absalom's feelings and attitudes.

Use impromptu Scripture (Bible character) interpretation at this point as you are helping class members to "get inside" Absalom. You are leading the class to explore thoroughly how Absalom felt, why he felt that way, and whether he could have felt any other way. Ask two of your most interested, capable members to impersonate Absalom and David for a few minutes. This is the situation which the two persons are to interpret: David has called Absalom to Jerusalem by secret messenger just as Absalom has all in readiness to attack his father. The two are seated in a private room in the palace. David leads off the conversation as he seeks reconciliation with his son. Absalom responds at first in a resentful tone and lists his chief grievances. David replies. Then both of them bring their deepest feelings out into the open. Reconciliation is achieved and civil war is averted.

After explaining this situation, ask the two members to begin their interpretive conversation. Each member will try to remain true to what he knows his biblical character feels. Yet he will move gradually (in four or five exchanges) to reconciliation. Allow two or three minutes for this imagined conversation as "Absalom" and "David" put their past failures behind them and start out again on a new relationship.

Interrupt the drama, then, and help the class to analyze the interpretations. Considering first "Absalom" and then "David," did they remain true enough in character to keep the imagined conversation in the realm of credibility? If not, why could not Absalom have said this or that? (Concentrate on Absalom.) If Absalom could have brought himself to feel—how?—then could he have spoken as he was interpreted? In short, what must Absalom have felt in order for reconciliation to have been achieved at that time between him and his father?

Concluding the Study

Now you are ready to help members to think seriously and wholly about their own feelings toward one or both parents. Use *circular response* in order to encourage each person to respond thoughtfully and individually to the study situation. Ask members to reflect silently for a whole minute upon this question: What can one do to develop more feeling of appreciation and respect for his parents? After at least a full sixty seconds of reflection, start with a responsive member and go from one person to the next around the class securing suggestions. Do not bypass anyone unless he insists on not responding. Urge good group sportsmanship, the need for everyone's ideas, and so on. Write in a column on the chalkboard or discussion board the key word or phrase in each idea for inner change. As with brainstorming, accept and record without evaluation all suggested solutions to this spiritual problem.

Each class member now has offered at least one way in which a person can change his feelings toward deeper respect for parents. If time allows and you sense that the class mood is right for this further process, lead members to suggest a chronological order for the ideas they have offered. With the chalkboard, simply place numbers before the ideas in the order in which members agree that the personal actions for inner change should take place. With the discussion board, move the cards around into the order which members agree is best. (The discussion board thus is a portable, dustless, chalkboard!)

Up to this point, you still have not confronted your individual class member with what *he* will do in order to develop a deeper conviction about respect for parents. Every person will not want to start with the idea listed first on the chalkboard. He will not want to follow the sequence which the class has agreed upon as seeming spiritually profitable. And so you use *reflection-prayer* to help each person face himself and his God on this matter. Ask members to ponder and pray briefly over this question: What will *I* do this week in order to develop a deeper feeling of appreciation and respect for that parent for whom I need this feeling most? As the class period ends, lead in prayer for the Holy Spirit's guidance and prompting for yourself and for each other class member.

7
Feature Forums

Not only can a forum be built around some relatively informal activity. A definite assignment type of feature may become the key activity that launches and unifies a forum-kind of learning session. Several major varieties are described in this chapter. You, as an imaginative teacher, may adapt these to your needs or discover other kinds of features that you can use in leading Bible study.

Assignment-Report Forum

Your teaching aim will determine the kind of assignment you make when using the assignment-report forum. If your aim for class members is Bible knowledge, then you may assign members to do Bible and other research, to complete workbook or programed learning assignments, and the like. If you are aiming at understanding and appreciation of Bible content, you may assign interviews, reflection, experiments, and so on. With aim III (conviction), the assignment may involve experiments, conversations or interviews with others, and reflection coupled with earnest prayer. In the last case, the assignment is more of a mutually-arrived-at covenant than any assignment from you to members, of course. With such an application of Bible truth to life aim (aim IV), the assignment, as with aim III, may be experiment or other activity which involves actually doing what you and class members have agreed you should and want to do.

We are using aim I in this instance: *To help class members to examine the experiences of Absalom and David as they show the relationship of the two as son and father.*

Beginning the Study

Perhaps you will use a stimulating way of tying in this session with the preclass session. Members may need this or another kind of emotional involvement in order to respond best to a session devoted to gaining Bible facts.

Probably this session begins a unit of study on biblical insights into son/daughter-parent relationships. Members will be helped by knowing that the significance of the Bible facts they are about to discuss will continue to increase as the unit of Bible study develops out of this foundation-laying session. As you use *lecture* to preview the unit briefly, challenge members to help discover, in this first session, absolutely every biblical fact which they will need in any other session of the unit. This demand upon members' foresight and intellectual awareness can help them to reach that state of mental alertness and interest you desire.

At the last session, you assigned specific questions either to individual persons or to the whole class. (Individual assignments seem better. Personal responsibility and less work per person are some of the benefits of this plan.) Questions were written down and numbered —for clarity's sake, as reminders, for easier follow-up, and for other good reasons. Besides, you could use your copy of these same questions in calling for reports at the next session.

The questions which you gave to the class covered the biblical story of Absalom and David as thoroughly as you could phrase them to do. In fact, they dealt with more details in the life of David than you might have tried to cover had you used one of the other teaching aims; for, with those aims, your purpose would have become more selective. You might have needed fewer details at this place and that in the life of David. Or at least you would have dealt with them more quickly and in the way which best served your study plans.

In this case, using aim I, details were your objective! So you asked members to trace David's marriages, his children, his wars, his sins, his signs of affection for Absalom, his attitude toward God, and so on. You assigned members to use their Bible dictionaries, concordances, and so on, and to look up and bring to class every recorded fact about Absalom and every interpretation of Absalom's life events which reliable commentators have provided. Even if members had only Bibles and concordances, though, they were shown how to do a good job of Bible searching.

Write numbers on the chalkboard in a column representing the questions you assigned. Now, starting with question 1, ask members to report the Bible information they have gathered. Although these questions were numbered for easy reference, remember that they were listed as they came first into your mind. There is no really accurate chronological order to them at present. And so if some member is absent or has failed to secure the answer to his question, move on to the next question. You and the class simply are getting before you on the chalkboard all of the Bible information which members have discovered during the week. You probably would be wise, moreover, to ask a good writer to copy from the board what you are writing. This valuable data might get erased before your next session!

When you have written on the chalkboard all the biblical information which class members can offer, help members to identify what is lacking. Your copy of the questions perhaps is your best checklist. Give Bible dictionaries or other reference books to members who have participated least so far, and help them to find the information that is missing. You have looked up all of this scriptural data yourself, of course, as preparation for this session. Give enough leads at this stage of Bible study for other class members also to be searching in their Bibles for the missing facts. You can ask some members to be verifying facts that you think are in error. Give them Scripture references to use in this verification. Although this Bible searching phase of the class session is valuable, do not allow it to drag. More is to be done and time is short.

Going Further in Bible Study

Now your biblical data is complete. If your time schedule allows, *divide the class* in half. Ask each small group to gather in a circle. Then request Group 1 to arrange the top half of the chalkboard list of facts and events in the best chronological order they can. Ask Group 2 to do the same with the bottom half of the list. Each group chooses a chairman and goes to work.

The chairman leads discussion and records the ordering of events as members agree item by item. You can see the value of this procedure in helping members to become aware of what the facts were in the lives of Absalom and David. Also, a knowledge of the general chronological order of events is needed by members for the sessions to come. If time is short, do not use the small-group study. Simply help the class rearrange the chalkboard list in the best order they (and you) can agree upon. Don't bother to rewrite anything. Simply renumber the events at the end of the lines and this is your chronological order.

If you have used small-group study, call the class back into the larger circle as quickly as they have finished. Ask the chairmen to report the groups' decisions. Write the new series of numbers at the end of the lines of data. As you record one group's opinion about biblical sequence, ask if other members accept this thinking. Using your own previous research, you of course may assist in this process of verification wherever you are needed.

Now hand out paper and pencils to members as you prepare to use *Scripture paraphrasing* to help teach the Bible facts. Ask each person to write a paragraph of some five to ten sentences giving his own factual account of Absalom's brief life from birth to death—including David's lament. Discourage judgments about Absalom and David where you can do so without hurting freedom of participation. For you and the class will be pursuing an understanding aim in the next session. Allow three or four minutes for this writing. Collect these *unsigned* summaries of Bible biography, mix them up well, and read one or two at random. Save these sheets for your own study and possibly for reference later in the unit.

Concluding the Study

Use brief *lecture* to make your own quick summary of events in the lives of Absalom and David. Mention any other facts which need researching before the next session, assigning responsibility to members or assuming this yourself. Select one or two situations that seem difficult to understand and spotlight these as problems for members to be thinking hard about in preparation for the next session. A question like this is an example: Looking at it from his viewpoint, was Absalom really wrong in thinking that he should inherit the throne? Then remind members that deeper levels of study thus are before them which will require frequent review of and reflection upon the facts discussed in this section.

Debate Forum

The debate forum fosters a "high temperature" class session. Usually it helps you best with a "low temperature" topic. If class members are bored with the subject of child-parent relationships, this approach to Bible study encourages energetic thinking and emotional involvement. Select the debate question carefully so that discussion on it carries the class right to the heart of the topic's biblical truth. The achieving of your teaching aim follows closely thereafter. Your object with this method is not to "settle" the question, but to stimulate intensive thought on Bible truth as it helps with child-parent relationships. Since you are hoping for inner change and conviction to result from this warm-spirited study session, teaching aim III seems appropriate as a guide to teach by: *To help class members, in light of the experiences of Absalom and David, to strengthen their convictions about respecting and loving their parents.*

Beginning the Study

Use *lecture* to tie in naturally with the preclass session, if this earlier period was planned in order to help prepare for Bible study. Relate this topic to those which have preceded in the unit.

Then use an *unsigned, written survey of the class* to focus members' minds sharply and immediately upon a chief issue in this study. Hand out pencils and slips of paper and ask each person to write, unsigned, his answer to this question: What is the one strongest point you can give in defense of Absalom, before our debate begins? Actually, these responses can serve as a presession test to help you later as you evaluate the quality of class advance study. But this is not your chief purpose for the procedure. Its contribution to class study appears later in these paragraphs. As soon as brief phrases or sentences have been written by everyone, collect the responses and place them on the table for later use. Assure members that their written arguments soon will play an important role in the Bible study session.

Now use *lecture* to set quickly the biblical sequence leading up to the emergence of Absalom in the story of David and the kingdom: Some historical facts leading up to David's marriages with heathen princesses probably are sufficient. You are depending upon your debaters and subsequent classroom procedures under your leadership to "teach the Bible" and the "lesson" as everyone comes to grips with biblical statements and meanings.

Introduce the debate now. Introduce the two (or four) class members who have prepared thus to lay the basis for class study. State the question for debate, which may be something like this: "*Resolved:* That a person's only hope of achieving his real selfhood is to make a complete break with his parents." Say who will use Bible facts about Absalom and David to argue the affirmative; who, the negative.

Explain that each side will have from five to eight minutes to make continuous, new points. If you use only two debaters, the affirmative speaks for about three minutes, then the negative for three minutes. No rebuttal is allowed. If you use four speakers, the affirmative speaks first, then the negative, then the affirmative, and finally the negative, all for two minutes each. These four are to keep introducing new Bible facts and new logic, with as little refuting of previous statements as possible.

Your next processes will take care of the rebuttal (and the "judging"). Here you want as much Bible data and interpretation as possible to come before the class. Alert the rest of the class to evaluate carefully facts and arguments on both sides of the question. Assure them that they will need this balanced background when the debate is over.

Introduce the first debater and ask other debaters to follow in their turn without your interruption. As moderator of the debate, you should intervene only if requested to do so by one of the debaters or if circumstances clearly indicate that you should do so. Be ready quickly to provide a Bible or to render similar assistance if requested.

Going Further in Bible Study

Now the brief debate is over. The issue of son/daughter-parent relationship has been struck sharply. And most of the details concerning Absalom's relationship to his father hopefully have been established in the thinking of the class.

Perhaps this is the time for us to pause and say that everything which has occurred up to this point could have taken place in a preclass session or opening assembly. Two or more classes making up this larger group then could have moved to their classrooms and proceeded to follow up on the debate as we are about to outline. If two debaters of considerable Bible knowledge had handled the affirmative and negative in this preclass period, then you would have been using a form of *team teaching* for this study.

Now, *divide the class* into two groups either by simply marking off the class in half or by arranging them for maximum small-group thinking and participation. Ask Group 1, who are "for" Absalom, quickly to do three things: (1) Evaluate the negative side's use of biblical facts and supply any supporting Bible facts which the affirmative side overlooked. (2) Evaluate the logic of the negative speakers and write down any weaknesses discovered. (3) List briefly the best arguments made by the affirmative speakers. The affirmative debaters meet with Group 1 as resource persons, but the discussion leader (and later reporter for the group) is one who was not in the debate.

Group 2 is "for" the father, David. These members quickly will do these things: (1) Evaluate the affirmative side's use of the Scriptures and supply any supporting Bible facts which the negative side overlooked. (2) Evaluate the logic of the affirmative speakers and write down any weaknesses discovered. (3) List briefly the best arguments made by the negative speakers. The negative debaters meet with this group, again merely as resource persons and not to influence actively the group's decisions.

Allow about ten minutes for small-group discussion. Admittedly this is a short time for satisfying group deliberation. If you have more time available, all the better. But what does not receive sufficient discussion in small groups can be dealt with in the group-reporting period. Moreover, always remember that you can substitute large-group discussion for the small-group procedure, using the same questions.

Call now for the discussion leader from Group 1 to tell what his members decided about each part of their assignment. Write these statements on the chalkboard by number under the heading "Group 1." At this point, read aloud the responses from the unsigned slips and (pleasantly) compare these with Group 1's statements. How well prepared were class members before the debate began? In a parallel column under the heading "Group 2," write by number this group's evaluation of the affirmative side. Then lead the class briefly in comparing the opinions of the two groups. Seek to help members arrive at an agreement that the negative side of the question contains the most compelling arguments. Absalom's fate—and David's grief?—indicate that this is so.

Concluding the Study

Now use *brainstorming* to help members give expression to what they feel about their own respect for parents. Ask a question like this: How may I achieve independence and self-respect while cultivating a deeper feeling of respect for my parents? Use a discussion board to record responses. As each suggested solution to this spiritual problem is offered, write the key word or phrase on a 4 by 6 card with crayon and slip it into the lengthwise slot on the discussion board. If you think that members will be reluctant to begin offering ideas, use *circular response* rather than brainstorming.

After members have suggested, with your help, all the answers possible to your question, take the cards from the discussion board. Pass the stack of cards around quickly, starting half of them at each end of the class. Invite each member to take the card bearing a suggestion which he thinks has possibilities for him to act upon. At least, the card can act as a reminder to him that he definitely feels some way or other about achieving a deeper respect and affection for his parents. Use *reflection-prayer* as you ask members to consider themselves and their parents, and God's power to guide and inspire them.

Test Forum

This type of feature forum may be used to bring out important Bible facts and to stimulate reflection upon Bible meanings. Used in a serious but gamelike fashion, test forum encourages class members to exert maximum effort in gaining Bible information and in understanding its meaning for their lives. Thus the procedure is excellent for achieving teaching aim II, and this is the aim we are working toward here: *To help class members understand and appreciate the significance of the experiences which Absalom and David had as son and father.*

Beginning the Study

Use *lecture* to relate this Bible study to the preclass session and to the whole unit of study. This method is relatively "low temperature" as far as arousing the emotions is concerned. Thus you may need to highlight the relevance of this topic through use of a provocative newspaper article or other statement, a disturbing question out of the everyday lives of class members, or the like. Do this, that is, unless the earlier period accomplished this learning readiness for you. A chart assists you well in tying this early topic into the unit.

Now use *lecture* again for about two minutes to carry the Bible account from where you have just left it in your unit clarification to where David marries Absalom's mother. This generally is the historical point at which your test for this study begins. Members may range backward from this time in their answers, of course.

You are almost ready to hand out duplicated copies of the test. Class members understand, from your previous planning to use this procedure, that the test is to be worked at quite seriously. But they know that your main object is not to test their knowledge. Rather, it is to increase their knowledge, to deepen their understanding of and appreciation for God's Word, and to form a basis for deeper study. You have prepared the test carefully and prayerfully. Members find question 1 perhaps asking them to look at a jumbled list of events in the lives of Absalom and David. Each person is to arrange these events in chronological order simply by placing numbers in the correct sequence beside the particular events, regardless of where the events appear on the printed list.

Other questions use the biblical information differently. Question 2 perhaps asks members to list briefly the injuries which David inflicted upon Absalom. Question 3 asks for the listing of the injuries which Absalom inflicted upon David. Question 4 may call for each person to list and *number* the occasions in the story when relationships between Absalom and David might have been repaired. And question 5 asks each member first to copy in a column the numbers used in question 4. Then he writes two sentences beside each number. One sentence states what David might have done on that occasion to try to restore relationships. The other sentence states what Absalom might have attempted in order to achieve reconciliation. You have left plenty of room after each question on the sheet for members to respond as the test requests.

Now hand out pencils and copies of the test. You already have arranged tables, writing boards, or other surfaces to work on. Members may use their Bibles occasionally, but Bible searching and verification largely is part of the later forum period. The class is to take the test primarily on the basis of their advance study. Therefore, allow about ten or fifteen minutes for the test. You want to use most of the class period for verifying answers and discussing interpretations.

Going Further in Bible Study

When members have finished the test, you lead in stating the correct answers. On question 1, for instance, you may use *circular re-*

sponse as one person and then the next gives the order in which events occurred in the Absalom-David relationship. Part of the interest and depth of learning come as members question one another's answers. Insist in a friendly spirit that questioners prove their points by Bible chapter and verse. On really difficult questions, help them out, for you have worked out the best set of answers you could, in advance. Remain open and modest, however. Someone in class may prove you wrong! A discussion board, perhaps called in this case a "storyboard," aids clarity if you take cards with the events already written on them and arrange them on the board according to the class's decisions.

Circular response is a convenient and democratic way to lead class Bible study throughout the correcting of the test. And each member checks his own paper. But helping members to arrive at correct answers to questions 2–5 becomes more difficult—and more rewarding. For here your class members are working their own needs and feelings into their answers. For instance, one has to decide what "injure" means to him before he is through listing the ways in which Absalom injured his father. And for one to explain to the rest of the class why he listed a certain act of David which others overlooked immediately adds a new dimension to the Bible study.

Watch your time during this phase of the class session, for ten minutes are yet needed for the class to discuss thoughtfully question 5. This deliberation climaxes the Bible study session. Here members reflect upon the importance and potential which lie in the week-by-week contacts between son or daughter and parents.

Concluding the Study

Close with one minute of *reflection-prayer*. Ask members to think about what is taking place *now* in relationships with their parents. Invite each person to pray silently about this relationship as the period ends.

Book Review Forum

You may discover an excellent book or other form of literature which deals with the scriptural account of Absalom and David. The writing may propose to be a biblical study of this son and father, or it may seek to discuss son-father relationships using these two biblical characters for illustration. While a book treatment is the form of literature we are considering here, you may use much the same procedures when using play reading or poetry study. You still are going to relate to your Scripture passages whatever writing you use, for you are still leading Bible study, even with this type of feature forum.

Moreover, we assume here that you are using *lecture* as you review the book for the class. But you may use *assignment-report* and involve one or more members in presenting the book data to the class. If you ask another teacher to play this role, you are using *team teaching* in your total approach. The book review may come during the preclass session or opening assembly, using team teaching or another procedure. Or, the study may take place in your class session.

The kind of book we are using is thoroughly Bible based, and may even be an exposition of selected passages. Thus this review with its accompanying procedures assist you well in achieving teaching aim I. We are using this knowledge aim here: *To help class members examine the experiences of Absalom and David in their relationship as son and father.*

Beginning the Study

Relate your study naturally to the preclass session if this period was planned to support the study. Since book review forum may be a rather "low temperature" teaching approach, highlight its significance if a prior period did not do this.

Then use a chart or *lecture,* alone, to show how this first session in the unit relates possibly to the studies which have preceded and prepares specifically for those to follow. You may explain how the factual approach used here lays the foundation for deeper understandings and commitments later in the unit.

Remind the class of the Bible survey *assignment* which you gave them during the last session. You asked each member to review carefully the whole biblical account of Absalom and David. You appointed two persons to become the "chief guardians" of the Scripture record during this session. They were to examine the Bible account so thoroughly that they could serve as resource persons in class discussion.

You are ready now to introduce the book, its author, and any other significant information. Circumstances, of course, determine the amount of detail you give in your review; the time factor controls your decision to a great degree. But, in any event, for about twenty minutes do justice both to the book and to the other procedures that are planned. Allow the book to play a role important and helpful enough to justify using this procedure. Help it to succeed in laying the framework for further thoughtful Bible study.

Going Further in Bible Study

Now look closely with the class at the facts and interpretations which the review book has made. *Divide the class* into two groups, and place in each group one of your specially prepared resource persons. Request each group to select a leader-reporter, someone other than the Bible resource person.

Ask group members to use their Bibles and other resource materials to prepare written responses to these questions: (1) In what ways do we question the biblical facts and interpretations of the book which has been reviewed? (2) What events and other items of Bible information have special importance for understanding Absalom and David as son and father? (3) (For Group 1 only) From the facts about Absalom which we have examined, the young man in which portrait looks the most like Absalom? Explain.

Remind the resource person in each group that he has prepared in such a way as to be of special help on question 1. He is the "guardian" of the Bible facts concerning Absalom and David, and is to lead the group in answering this question fully. Encourage each study leader to secure a carefully prepared list, from parentage to David's lament, in answer to question 2. With question 3 you are using *picture study* to help members become intellectually and emotionally involved with the biblical facts that describe Absalom. (Turn back to the discussion above of picture study with small-group study forum for helpful details on using this teaching method.) Allow the small groups about fifteen minutes to carry out their Bible verification and other study assignments.

Then regroup the class in a circle and call for group reports. In column 1 on the discussion board or chalkboard, write all points of questioning from first Group 1 and then Group 2. Occasionally compare the thinking of the two groups. Don't attempt to defend the review book as reservations about facts and interpretations are expressed. Simply write down one or two key words from each point until every response concerning question 1 is before the class. Then lead the class to evaluate briefly each questioning response. Require that members use Bibles and other resource books in supporting their viewpoints.

Now ask for group answers to question 2. Using discussion board cards in recording responses to this question helps you in preserving this class-produced data for later studies in the unit. Again, compare or complement certain insights which a group offers.

Next call for Group 1 to explain what they were asked to do, and what they did, concerning portraits of "Absalom." When the reporter for Group 1 has finished, invite members of Group 2 to evaluate Group 1's decision. Encourage friendly difference of interpretation. There is no one answer, of course, and you want to encourage creative, reflective, readily expressed feelings concerning Absalom's outward characteristics. Thus members begin to identify more fully with their counterpart in David's household.

Concluding the Study

You will now want to help members summarize clearly in their minds the Bible facts explored in this session. Use a *written survey of the class* and *Scripture paraphrasing* for this purpose. Hand out pencils and paper to each person. Request members to take three minutes to write a brief chronological account of the most significant events in the lives of Absalom and David as son and father. They may refer to the chalkboard, of course, selecting from this long list of events the most significant ones.

Then collect the sheets and read one aloud. Keep these biblical summaries, and after class select the best ones for review purposes later in the unit of study.

Before adjourning, ask members to be thinking of gaps in understanding which they have concerning Absalom's relationship with his father. State that in the next session you will be trying to discover all of these gaps in understanding as to what happened between Absalom and his father, what might have happened, whose fault it was, and so on. End the study with prayer for the Holy Spirit's enlightenment as members go more deeply into these Bible passages and their implications.

Audio-Visual Forum

This final type of feature forum usually requires about an hour for satisfying results. The preclass session, as in team teaching, often presents the audio-visual part of the Bible study. Thus you and other teachers may have the usual time in class for Bible analysis and intensive class evaluation of what has been presented in the first period. But you may use this approach totally within your own class.

We are about to look at four kinds of audio-visual teaching aids. Other audio-visual forms of presenting Bible study material may be adapted to what we see is possible with biblical films, contemporary films, and tape or disc recordings of biblical and contemporary material. We begin by imagining ourselves using a *Bible film* portraying the Absalom-David story. We follow our procedures partway through the session, then go back and discuss how our procedures may vary using other audio-visual aids. Again we pick up the classroom process, which now becomes the same for all four teaching media for the remainder of the session.

Audio-visual teaching aids assist in "raising the temperature" of class Bible study. The emotions are stirred and the mind becomes active. Thus we use this approach in seeking to achieve teaching aim III, which is concerned with forming convictions: *To help class members, in light of the experiences of Absalom and David, to strengthen their convictions about respecting and loving their parents.*

Beginning the Study

First, use *lecture* to remind members of the biblical setting in which they will view the film, relating this study to those which have preceded in the unit. State briefly how the film will take up the biblical account and assist in a careful study of the perplexing Absalom-David relationship.

You may want to use a supplementary approach which will foster maximum observation of and reflection upon the film. If so, appoint *reaction groups* from your class. This may be done right in the department or other large-group assembly, with other teachers possibly doing the same. If you are using the film only in your class, of course you have no procedural problem here. However, you may have appointed these reaction groups at the close of the last class session, with assignments given in writing; or you may have done this during the week by mail. However you make the assignments, though, you will still read all the questions to the group before showing the film. Thus everyone will know what is being looked for in the picture.

For the reaction groups, make four listening-reaction assignments *in writing.* Perhaps two members on each listening task are enough. With a class of only six persons, give one assignment to each of four persons. Ask the four groups or persons to view the film and be prepared to answer these questions: (1) What are the three best reasons given in the film why Absalom could justify his resentment and rebellion toward David? (2) What qualities did the film show David possessing which Absalom as a young man still could have respected enough to have built a satisfying relationship upon? (3) What son-parent problems did the film portray which hardly exist in family relationships today? (4) What child-parent problems exist today which the film did not show or imply? These questions help lay the foundation for thorough Bible study and reflection. Thus it is important for each reaction member to receive his question in writing for frequent reference before and immediately after the film.

Remind everyone of what is being looked for, and show the film. Under some circumstances, you may show the film twice if it is not too long. Class members may say that they need this reviewing in order to clarify certain facts or interpretations.

If you use a *tape* or *disc recording* of biblical data, you proceed much as you do with the biblical film. Perhaps you or someone in your class has written a *Scripture paraphrase* of the Absalom-David story. Or, this biblical data may be in simple play or drama form, and you and some of your class members have recorded this written dialogue or paraphrase for playing in this preclass or regular class session.

Absalom and David may be in conversation just before Absalom launches his rebellion. David is trying to persuade Absalom to change his course. Absalom brings up all the grievances he feels, with David replying after each complaint. Both speakers reflect the Scriptures as accurately as possible.

You may assign the same questions as with the biblical film. And since you and one or two selected class members prepared the recording after careful Bible research, the recording does contain helpful data for the use of your reaction groups. Play the recording while the reaction groups and others in the class listen for answers to the questions.

The *contemporary film* calls for a somewhat different approach. This film portrays problem situations in today's son/daughter-parent relationships. First, use *assignment-report* or *lecture* for about ten minutes, not only to review the biblical setting, but also to provide the class with the type of biblical background which we said the biblical recording involved.

The next step is to appoint six *reaction persons* or *groups*. Each group receives one of these questions to answer as members view the film and reflect later upon what they saw: (1) What son-parent situations were similar in both the Absalom-David relationship and in the film? (2) What son-parent situations were different in one story from the other? Explain. (3) What son characteristics were similar in both the biblical account and in the film? (4) What son characteristics were different in one story from the other? Explain. (5) What father characteristics were similar in both accounts? (6) What father characteristics were different in each account? Explain.

Now show the contemporary film. If members request a reshowing for clarity and the film is not too long, rerun the picture.

You may be using a *contemporary sound recording* for this first phase of Bible study. Perhaps you have located a penetrating one-act play on son-parent relationships appropriate for your class members. Or you and one or two of your members have written a script tailor-made to your members' own concerns. This script may resemble the kind of dialogue which occurs in good role playing. In fact, you may have recorded some role playing between a resentful "son" and a neglectful "father" by two class members for this very purpose.

Assign questions like the following to each of four reaction persons or groups: (1) How do you describe or characterize the father in the recording? (2) How do you describe or characterize the son in the recording? (3) In what ways was David different from the audio father? (4) In what ways was Absalom different from the audio son? Now play the recording once or twice while reaction groups listen carefully for possible answers to their questions. Other members are noting everything they can, and perhaps "checking up" on the reaction group which is of particular interest to them.

Going Further in Bible Study

You now have provided the biblical setting and shown the film or played the recording once or twice. Allow about three minutes for reaction groups and other members to remain where they are and reflect silently upon the best answers to their questions. Then, if this first phase of Bible study has been a preclass or opening assembly period, adjourn the large group to their classes or divide into small groups.

Now call for reactions to the film or recording. After Group 1 has taken two or three minutes to report, invite other class members to react to what has just been said in answer to question 1. From your own careful preparation, guide this discussion and the evaluation of other reports. Remember your number III teaching aim (conviction) throughout the remainder of the session. Take up the questions and reaction group reports in the order you gave them out. From time to time, when the discussion strays too far from the question being analyzed, remind members of questions coming up very soon. Straight and intense thinking upon Bible concepts is one of your aims with this study process.

As soon as you and the class have considered the reaction group reports to the general satisfaction of the class, use *brainstorming*. Build upon what the class has considered so far by stating a key problem in understanding the Absalom-David relationship. Ask for solutions to this question: What were some of the good chances for Absalom and David, in the months preceding Absalom's death, to become closer and more respecting of each other? As class members think through this question, they begin to move toward the idea of achieving this more respecting relationship with their own parents.

Encourage the naming of every conceivable occasion when Absalom and David could have had good chances to move toward reconciliation. Write each response on a card for the discussion board or list suggestions on the chalkboard. When members and you, also, have explored briefly and listed all possibilities, lead the class to rank these potential occasions for reconciliation in the order of their probability. That is, ask which occasion offered the best chance for the two; which the next best chance; and, finally, which was the least likely opportunity for reconciliation. Simply rearrange the cards in the order the class prefers, or number the chalkboard list in the order the class agrees upon.

Now use *reflection* and *circular-response* to help members go more deeply into the matter of Absalom's real problems with his father. Ask a question like this: Why may Absalom have been unable to respect and draw closer to his father? Request members to reflect silently for two minutes upon this question, considering all that has been said so far about Absalom. Now the main concern is the son and his feeling for David.

After two minutes of class reflection, use circular response to secure from each person the results of this important thinking. Call on a member who is likely to respond willingly and thoughtfully to begin the speculation. Then move from one member to another around the class. List these responses in a second column on the chalkboard. You will have good reason to refer to some of these feelings in the next phase of Bible study. Take three or four minutes to help the class pick out those possible "reasons" of Absalom's which seem most unjustified.

Concluding the Study

Here you are ready to lead members in considering their own feelings of respect for parents, in light of the Bible study thus far. Use an *unsigned written survey* of the class to secure the most frank, creative ideas possible. You are close, with the Holy Spirit's help, to achieving your teaching aim if members respond willingly and thoughtfully at this point.

Distribute pencils and paper to each class member. See that everyone has something to write on. Then ask each member to write, unsigned, his one best answer to this question: What can a son [or daughter, if you are teaching young women] do to develop in his heart more feeling of respect for his parents? Allow two or three minutes for members to reflect upon the question and to jot down a few words describing their ideas. While the class is pondering this question, prepare to use the chalkboard to record answers from the written responses.

Now collect the slips of paper, mix them up to insure anonymity, read each response, and record it in a third column on the chalkboard. If important possibilities are overlooked by class members, supply these or lead members in thinking of them. Refer the class to reasons listed in column 2 for additional ideas. When all possibilities for inner change are listed before the class, lead members to arrange these ideas in something of a chronological order. For instance, if "prayer" and "talk with my parent" are listed, perhaps members will say that prayer should precede specific, direct actions. Do not encourage technical, dogmatic arguing in this process of thinking through a sequence. Maybe you should use only five minutes for this kind of reflection upon the list of action possibilities.

As the class period is about to end, use *reflection-prayer*. Ask each class member if he will think quietly of the possibilities which have been discussed as to how to develop in one's heart a deeper feeling of respect for parents. Call attention, also, to the reasons the class members have given as to why Absalom may have been his own worst enemy in the tragic relationship with his father. Wait a full minute before ending the silent reflection and prayer with your own audible prayer for Christ's guidance and support for you and the class.

Words of Counsel

You may be thinking how easy and natural all of these teaching procedures sound, but how hard it will be to use them with spiritual profit! Practice will increase the ease with which you teach in these stimulating ways. Meanwhile, be adaptable. Always be ready to adjust to the time factor or to other changes in the classroom situation. Make no special apology; do not act as if your teaching plans are wrecked.

Eliminate a certain procedure cheerfully and perhaps unannounced. If the shortness of time prevents your using role playing as you had planned, continue the class session with a thought-provoking question and unsigned written responses or another procedure which achieves your purpose to a large extent. Study these teaching approaches and become fully conscious of what each one uniquely contributes to provoking class thought and exploration, analysis, and interpretation of the Bible. Then, after some practice with these study processes, you will learn to substitute easily.

To illustrate further, you may use the less time-consuming brainstorming for circular response or small-group discussion. You may use individual classroom Bible research and reflection for small-group study. Reaction groups can substitute for the longer debate forum if you make the reaction group assignments appropriately. Use written survey of the class in place of small-group study, role playing, or circular response. Substitute brainstorming and lecture for formal discussion. Informal discussion can take the place of many other procedures, including formal discussion, test forum, and colloquy, if your questions are phrased well. Remember that small-group study and panel forum make up the colloquy; divide the colloquy into substitute approaches when circumstances require it. Lecture can take the place of book review. And role playing can substitute for a film.

Also, creatively adapt the teaching approaches described briefly here. Use book review forum on a more extended time scale. Or raise the "temperature" of class sessions which are failing to involve members mentally and emotionally. Having become thoroughly familiar with the key idea of each procedure, suddenly employ role playing to help members realize the relevance of an important Bible truth. Or, as the Holy Spirit gives you presence of mind, pause and announce that the next phase of class study calls for debate on the biblical interpretation being discussed.

Arouse the personal interest of members by using unsigned written responses all of a sudden. If you are having trouble securing class concentration upon some Bible truth, ask for feelings concerning its most personally-involving implication. Once the penetrating importance of the passage is highlighted this way, class Bible study suddenly becomes interesting and dynamic to members. Each person discovers that he *is* personally involved, more than he had admitted, in what God's Word says and means.

8
Evaluating Class Bible Study

You prepare thoroughly to guide the class in Bible study. You feel that you do your best in leading the class in thoughtful study and response to Bible truth. Yet you feel, somehow, that your task is not finished. What more is there to do?, you ask. There *is* one thing more to do—*evaluate.*

The kind of teaching which you have been doing may be quite different from what you and your class were used to. You undertook these new classroom procedures with the best of spiritual intentions. You are confident that your class entered into these new approaches to Bible study with the holiest of desires, both toward your teaching responsibilities and toward their need to learn. Now you want to know if all the study and all the growing pains in learning new ways to teach are worthwhile. And your members want to know if they have just been playing games, or if they are learning really more serious and profitable ways to study the Scriptures.

It is quite natural for you to wonder how thought-provoking and effective your new teaching approaches are. And it is understandable that your class members want to know if all these new ways of Bible study are really more life-changing than lecture and listen. The way you and your class answer these questions is to pause and look at what you have done. A ship takes its bearings when passing through a critical channel. A space craft continually provides feedback to the guidance system which keeps the craft continuing toward its objective. Likewise, you and your members take stock. You take your bearings to see if everything about your Bible study together is working out as you and the class had planned.[1]

---

[1] See, also, John T. Sisemore (comp.), *Vital Principles in Religious Education* (Nashville: Broadman Press, 1966), pp. 111–18.

Why Evaluate?

Evaluation serves useful purposes other than answering your questions about how effective your teaching has been. For one thing, your stewardship of the written Word *requires* that you take notice of what effect your teaching is having upon the class session and upon the lives of your members. Moreover, to take notice of what is happening to all of you, periodic attention to class procedures and study results is essential. How far off course will a guided missile go if its feedback mechanism is not used?

You have another reason, from your standpoint as teacher, for continuing to examine your teaching processes and their consequences. As you evaluate, you sharpen the goals which you and the class have accepted for Bible study. You make your objectives more specific. You revise them in order to achieve the maximum spiritual profit.

And, finally, you as teacher evaluate because this procedure is a sound and practical way to guide you toward achieving the spiritual goals which you determined for yourself when you accepted this trust. You will not try to evaluate those results of Bible study which cannot be evaluated with profit. But you are on solid educational ground to look closely at the many observable results which do appear.

You can count on the willing participation of your class members in evaluation if you present this matter to them in the right way. They, too, possess a deep desire to avoid "shadowboxing" when it comes to studying God's Word. They want to experience the real thing, a true encounter with the Scriptures.

Moreover, your members may be new to the experience of using varied classroom procedures. They want to know how well they are doing and where they need to improve. Many in your class are in the business world, where they have come to appreciate the need for taking periodic inventory.

And, finally, some of your members are mentally enough alert to be interested—perhaps intrigued—with this idea of purposefulness in Bible study. They like this idea of actually taking a look now and then to see if they can observe any change in themselves, anything happening anywhere as a result of their making such a place in their lives for organized, thoughtful Bible study. And they may be a little bit curious as to how this evaluation can be done.

Evaluate What?

As you and your class consider evaluating your Bible study experiences, remember that you are not able to measure every possible result. You do not even set out to do this.[2] But there will be noticeable results of one kind or another growing out of your study experiences. You can reflect upon these results. Different levels of evaluation are possible. These can be valid when used carefully and reflectively.

You and your class may approach the evaluation of your Bible study experiences in several ways. Here we think of evaluating a particular teaching-learning procedure, and then a whole unit of Bible study. As we go from the simpler to the more complex Bible study situation, we shall not develop again what already has been said. We simply shall refer to earlier statements, when helpful, and introduce new elements in the class experience that you and the class may want to evaluate.

A single procedure.—You had an outcome in mind when you planned and later used a particular teaching procedure in class. This procedure was to play a special role at a certain time during the session. Or, if it was a basic procedure running through virtually the whole period, it was used to aid you and the class in achieving the outcomes that you both desired.

Now you wish to evaluate this procedure and decide how or whether you will use it again. Ask yourself questions like these: (1) Did I *prepare* sufficiently in order to use this procedure to its best advantage? (Did I study the theory and use of the method as competent writers and teachers have described them? Did I seek the Holy Spirit's aid in this new venture for honoring God through leading stimulating Bible study? And so on.) (2) Did I *use* this method in class in such a manner that it could work its best for the class? (3) Did the procedure actually *make its unique contribution* to class Bible study? (4) Did the procedure seem to *cause any change* in members toward the achieving of my larger teaching aim or of a subaim?

Your class members also have much at stake in this procedure. They are taking these new study approaches seriously. Therefore, you

[2] See D. Campbell Wyckoff, *Theory and Design of Christian Education Curriculum* (Philadelphia: The Westminster Press, 1961), pp. 68–70.

must help them make their own evaluation of this Bible study process. Members start, as you did, with thinking of what they expected from the procedure. This expectation forms much of the background from which the method is gauged fairly by the class.

Then your members ask themselves questions like these: (1) Did we feel its appropriateness as the teacher introduced this procedure and led us into it? (2) Did we participate in the study process with the spirit, understanding, and skill needed for the procedure to do its unique work best? (3) When the procedure was completed, had we felt its "dynamics"? (Did we have the same or a similar kind of learning experience that others seem to have had when using this study method?)

The class may think of other questions which they want to ask themselves about this Bible study process and how they used it.

A unit of study.—Your unit teaching aim helps to provide the framework within which you evaluate the whole unit of study. Usually you will teach from a number IV (action) unit aim. Keeping this objective in mind, ask yourself: (1) Was the unit long enough to allow satisfying teaching? (2) Was the unit long enough to allow successful class planning for follow-through upon Bible study? (3) Did I phrase my teaching aims so that I related the sessions of the unit in the most spiritually profitable way possible? (4) (If evaluating at the end of the first unit of study) Did I show improvement from session to session in teaching preparation? (5) (If evaluating at the end of the first unit of study) Did I show improvement from session to session in the use of various teaching procedures? (6) Did I achieve my unit teaching purpose?

The class, in their evaluation of the unit's Bible study experiences, should keep in mind what was understood at the beginning to be their purpose in studying the unit. And they should ask themselves questions like these: (1) Was the unit of Bible study satisfying mentally and spiritually? (2) Did we show improvement from session to session in individual advance preparation for class Bible study? (Did we improve in the *amount* of advance preparation we made? Did we improve in the *quality* of advance preparation; in the strength of thought applied to God's Word; in the amount and depth of reflection; in the types of sources consulted?) (3) (If evaluating at the end of the first unit of study) Did we show improvement from session to session in participating in classroom study procedures? (Did we encourage everyone in the class to play a part in Bible research and interpretation? Did we respond seriously to Bible study problems? Did we show fair play in class discussion? Did we show intellectual honesty in Bible interpretation and application? Did we show clear thinking in class discussion? Did we help keep discussion on the spiritual problem before the class at the moment?) (4) Did we actually become involved in *doing* that part of God's teaching which we agreed in class that we believed and wanted to give expression to in our daily living?

How to Evaluate

We have been talking in terms of the *process* of your Bible study and of its *results*. You and your class members will make the final decision as to what you will evaluate. You will also decide together how to go about examining and weighing the Bible study experiences which you and the class have engaged in. The methods or instruments you use in evaluating should provide the kind of information that helps you to judge results in terms of your aims. These instruments should be as accurate as you can make them. And they should be easy for you and the class to administer, score, and interpret.

Whatever evaluation you and the class make of your teaching and of members' activities in Bible study may constitute more purposeful, reflective checking up than you have ever done before. Your first steps in evaluation, therefore, can prove highly profitable and stimulating. When you reach that stage of desire and proficiency, you and your members can always move into involved types of evaluation. In the paragraphs to follow, we consider evaluation approaches which almost any thoughtful teacher and class can use, or simplify and adapt to their own needs.

Our approach to the question of *how* to evaluate class Bible study follows logically upon the way we considered *what* to evaluate. To answer the questions which you as teacher ask yourself about your use of a teaching procedure, we consider helpful evaluative approaches. Then we discuss how you help class members to weigh their own use of the procedure. (We do the same thing with the Bible study unit, using the same format for clarity's sake.)

Evaluating a Teaching Procedure

Evaluating as teacher.—Throughout this part of the chapter, we devote more space to class evaluation than to your evaluation as teacher. We do this partly because you share also in the class evaluation. We also do this because, if you go as far as is suggested for you here, you already will be well on the way toward more excellence in leading class Bible study. Moreover, later in the chapter we consider methods of securing class reaction to certain of the assessments you have made of your teaching.

When you consider all the ways for you and the class to evaluate any phase of class Bible study, you finally come back to three approaches: observation, interviewing, and paper and pencil methods.[3] As you look back on your handling of a procedure in class, use primarily (*1*) *reference to your teaching plans,* (*2*) *observation, and* (*3*) *reflection.* Examine your teaching plan sheet and your notes. What spiritual end was this procedure to accomplish? How had you planned to handle it? You may want to use brief essay style to describe what you decide. Save these notes for the time when you meet with class leaders or the whole class to compare reactions.

If you think that this full evaluation process with class members will occur some weeks from now, you may feel compelled to insert *interview* of one or two thoughtful class members after your own observation and before final reflection. You feel that you need counsel and support before the next class session! But if this evaluation of yours coincides with class evaluation and helps form part of a serious, scheduled class review process, secure your interview benefits as you and the class later compare notes.

Evaluating as class members. As indicated above under "Evaluate What?," there are several questions that class members need to face in order to evaluate a particular procedure. The first of these involves its appropriateness.

Use a *pro-con analysis* to secure oral class responses to this first question. Prepare to record answers in two columns on the chalkboard or discussion board. Head the two columns "appropriate" and "inappropriate." Ask members to name, as you write, the reasons

---

[3] See Miles, *op. cit.,* pp. 235–51.

why they felt that the procedure was quite appropriate, as it was introduced by you. Then list in column 2 any reasons members can offer against the procedure's seeming appropriate. Later in the evaluation process, you will call attention to the predominance of feeling for and against the procedure's appropriateness, and will lead the class to analyze helpful relationships between responses in the two columns.

Use of the discussion board with 4"x6" cards serves a useful purpose in this kind of class evaluation. Properly labeled, these cards are most convenient in later class analysis and in making decisions about what to do in future sessions.

A good way to help class members now and then to evaluate their participation in class Bible study is through use of a *tape recorder.* You can see the pointed effect of a class listening to themselves, noting this and that type of contribution.

After playing the recorder, you may ask for members' judgments about their *attitude,* their *understanding,* and their *skill* in the use of the procedure. Each member can write his own evaluation.

Having secured private reactions, you may want to use class *pro-con analysis* to explore the question more deeply. The "pro" question for column 1 may be, What all did we do that shows that we did participate as question 2 describes?

Instead of (or in addition to) the pro-con process, you and the class may want an objective evaluation. For example, a class member can be assigned to take notes on how others participate. This *observer* may use any one of several kinds of charts to record the quantity and quality of responses. For instance, he may have a sheet of paper listing the names of all class members on one side of the sheet. He then sits in the circle, or where he can see everyone else during use of the procedure, and writes a "1" by the name of each person every time he shows interest by making at least a *routine* response. He writes "2" beside a name each time that person makes a response that shows *understanding* of the procedure and what it is supposed to help the class do. The observer writes "3" beside a name each time that person responds with unusual *skill* in helping the procedure to work successfully.

Use a *linear rating scale* to help determine how individuals really were involved mentally and emotionally during the procedure. One end of the scale is labeled something like "Very much" and the other end, "Not at all." The middle number in the scale might read "Maybe a little." Number the scale 1-2-3-4-5 for members to circle.

Then use a total-group evaluation method like *pro-con analysis.* Employ the pro-con process either orally, using two columns on the discussion board, or in written form as an *open-end reaction sheet.* With the latter, more confidential approach, ask each member to write on his paper in one column the moving ideas and feelings he did have as a result of the procedure. He will write in a second column the ideas and feelings he expected, or thinks he should have had, but did not have. Collect the papers and save them for a later stage in this evaluation process.

Later in the chapter we shall discuss comparing this data with your own evaluation at points where they relate, and discussing variances with the class.

Evaluating a Unit of Bible Study

Evaluating as teacher.—You now move into evaluation which involves more perspective than you have dealt with previously. Perhaps you realize, moreover, that some of the checkup approaches already explored may be used with profit by you and the class when appraising a unit or a whole quarter's studies. Very probably you will make it a chief concern to weigh the degree to which you succeeded in leading the class in Christ-honoring actions in response to Bible study. Maybe a *notebook* kept by you and recording some of the details of these class decisions and activities will provide you with tangible results of this observation and reflection during the unit.

When you consider the question of improvement from session to session, you may want to supplement your own feelings with a *linear rating scale* from class members. These friends of yours surely are appropriate sources of research for you on the matter of your improvement in teaching skills. And they do not deal with this question directly in their research.

Evaluating as class members.—As given under "Evaluate What?," the first question for class members involves how satisfying the unit has been. Your members may not insist on separating "mentally" and "spiritually" in this question. There is a difference, but they appear here as mutually supporting. If members want to do so, you may use a *linear rating scale* with two levels: one concerning mental stimulation, and one, spiritual or emotional stimulation. Or use the scale with the question as it stands in "Evaluate What?"

Having secured confidential personal evaluations, use a *group evaluation process* to explore this first question more deeply. Ask members first to give evidences that the unit indeed was deeply satisfying. Write these responses in one column on the discussion board. Then encourage members to list reasons why the unit was not as satisfying as it might have been. List these points in column 2 as they are given. Or you can ask members to fill out a simple *questionnaire* which asks for this same yes-no evaluation in *open-end essay* fashion: "I felt that this unit was quite satisfying mentally and spiritually because———." Collect these evaluations for later analysis and planning.

You or the class president can secure further helpful measurement of success by privately *interviewing* two or three perceptive class members. Here you go beyond the bare question and ask *why.*

The second question involves members' improvement in preparation. This most certainly is one which class members need to answer for themselves, and a simple *questionnaire* will supply the information. Beforehand you will have done well to have made your own objective appraisal of this matter, based on *your classroom observation.* But now the members' reaction form may have three choices from which persons may check one: "Much improvement," "Maybe a little improvement," and "No improvement."

A *pro-con process* now goes further than the questionnaire and may show, with its more deliberative approach, some variances with the questionnaire tally. At least the questionnaire results will be interpreted partially by the results from this further instrument. Ask for classroom evidences which indicate decided improvement in quantity and in quality (distinguish on the discussion board). Then call for signs that very little improvement in advance preparation by members took place.

Now, consider the question of improved participation. Again place *your own objective observation* into the crucible of class evaluation. But keep your appraisal with you for the time being. Then use a *linear rating scale* to involve each member personally and most accurately in the review process.

Prearranged *observation by a class member* can produce valuable information regarding improved participation. He would need to have been assigned this task by the class at the beginning of the unit, of course. And he would have kept session by session notes, perhaps filled in after each session to avoid harming the spirit of the Bible study. Another class-appointed observer could have kept a *flow-of-individual-participation chart* from the beginning of the unit.

Are your members willing to be evaluated individually? If so, the class may choose an observer at the beginning of the unit. He is known in the class for his fair-mindedness and moderation! This person observes the roles which various members play in class discussion. Some members can be observed summarizing, clarifying, getting Bible study "back on the track," objecting to the teacher's interpretations, conciliating, disputing with members, dominating discussion, interrupting others, reading political overtones into any Bible analysis, always trying to discover "the true meaning of the verse," and so on.

A nonthreatening way to use this class-roles approach may be to call the process a "Guess Who?" checkup method. The class itself may prepare the list of roles. The observer then checks all of the behavior roles he sees demonstrated during the unit of study, and attaches names. When report and analysis time comes, he calls off, one by one, only the roles he has observed. The class tries to guess who is being described. Whether the observer reveals every time the name he has written beside the role may depend upon several factors of Christian love, maturity, and so on. But the value of the process is substantially retained, in any case.

A variation of this approach is for an observer to use a sheet bearing the names of all members. As each member makes a contribution to class discussion during the unit, this impartial and perceptive observer writes a qualitative symbol by the name. He may write, for an important contribution, +; for a moderately valuable comment, 0; for contributions of little value, −. Or the names may be left off and this observer may record only the assigned quality of each contribution.

When you come to the question of changed actions, *your own observation* of course is valid for later class consideration. Use a *simple ballot* calling for yes or no from class members. The class also may wish to *interview* concerned and thoughtful members about the degree of seriousness and reality with which members did become involved.

And, finally, members may want to check up at the other end of witness and ministry. The class may request two or three members to *interview outsiders* who have good reason to know how much genuine contact with human need was made by you and the class.

Reporting the Evidence

You and the class have filed in the correct envelopes or folders all the data that you gathered. You have kept your own observations separate. When you were helping the class to secure reactions in the various areas of evaluation, you did not even report the results from such instruments as the *linear rating scale* and the *open-end reaction sheet*. You and class members make these reports now.

Prepare the chalkboard, newsprint, or discussion board. Organize the recording area perhaps as an outline of the section, "Evaluate What?" Your large outline thus becomes: "A Teaching Procedure" and "A Bible Study Unit." Space questions under the two divisions far enough apart to record plainly the results which each checkup procedure reveals. You see that large sheets of newsprint or the discussion board has an advantage over the chalkboard here, if just for data preservation reasons.

Now call for reports of class evaluation. A little bit later, you bring into the picture certain results from your own appraisals as teacher, for comparison purposes. The class may have wished to distribute the reporting roles among several members. You should serve as discussion board recorder in order to give maximum help in interpreting results in the best form, in clarifying, in leading discussion on questionable points, and so on.

As soon as all class evaluations on the teaching procedure are tabulated accurately and recorded, add your own independent judgments at places where they apply. If you wrote these down and duplicated them, all the better. Distribute these results to all members for their quick observation and silent comparison with what they themselves have said. Then write your data on the discussion board. Repeat this whole process with the unit evaluation results.

Facing Up to the Evidence

Here is where the mind-stretching and heart-tugging become more intense. Starting with the data on using the special classroom procedure, help the class to compare the results from the various instruments and other evaluation procedures. For instance, how do the frank results from individual members on the *linear rating scale* for question 1 compare with the results from each of the other evaluation approaches? How do these other sets of results compare with one another? Which data may present the truest picture? Furthermore, how do your ratings at this point compare with the feelings of class members?

Continue this process of looking closely at all the results that you and the class have placed before you. Analyze variances. Try to explain honestly the differences that you cannot reconcile, and seek to understand why some data came in differently. Ask why a certain thing happened in the class study experiences. Could it have been avoided? Why? How?

Lead the class to ask and answer other questions like these: Did the changes in our knowledge, our understandings, our attitudes, and our actions come primarily as a result of the dynamic Bible study procedures which we used? Or were other influences more determinative? What were the other influences which affected our changes toward improvement or lack of improvement in the quality of our Bible study?

Deciding What to Do

Much of what you and the class have done is for the purpose of deepening your class Bible study experiences in the future. Lead the class now, therefore, to discover insights for future planning and use by *you* and the *class*. You might even group all insights into these two categories.

With the class, analyze in this manner all of the evaluation which you have done to this point. You may want to agree as teacher and class upon certain things that you are going to do differently from now on. This decision to seek improvement in the study of God's Word is the capstone of your evaluating process.

Be sure that your class undersands what evaluation involves before you encourage them to enter upon the experience. Set aside enough time to carry on the evaluation process in an unhurried, reflective fashion. Analyze the responses carefully. Some members unconsciously may not say what they think, but what they hope. Carry out the measurement procedures in a manner that does not threaten individuals. Your motive is to win and help, not to drive away.

INDEX

(*Bold numbers are major references.*)